Getting Started in
Six Sigma

The Getting Started in Series

Getting Started in
Six Sigma

Michael C. Thomsett

WILEY

John Wiley & Sons, Inc.

Published by John Wiley & Sons, Inc., Hoboken, New Jersey.
Published simultaneously in Canada.

For general information on our other products and services, or technical support, please contact our Customer Care Department within the United States at 800-762-2974, outside the United States at 317-572-3993 or fax 317-572-4002.

Wiley also publishes its books in a variety of electronic formats. Some content that appears in print may not be available in electronic books.

For more information about Wiley products, visit our web site at www.wiley.com.

Library of Congress Cataloging-in-Publication Data:

Thomsett, Michael C.
    Getting started in six sigma / Michael C. Thomsett.
       p.   cm.
    Includes index.
    ISBN 0-471-66811-7 (pbk.)
  1. Total quality management.   2. Six sigma (Quality control standard)
  I. Title.
    HD62.15.T524 2005
    658.4'013—dc22
2004013486

Printed in the United States of America.

10 9 8 7 6 5 4 3 2 1

Contents

Getting Started in
Six Sigma

Striving for Perfection in an Imperfect World

Is the goal within the organization to be *perfect* in every respect? Perfection is elusive, of course, but it can and does represent an enviable goal. More importantly, the concept of perfection helps everyone in the corporation to develop a working model to maximize excellent service at every level.

This is not a theory alone; the suggestion that you can work with other employees and managers to improve service is a crucial requirement in a competitive market. Thus, Six Sigma, as an integrated approach to creating effective working models, is much more than a tool for improving productivity, creating internal teamwork, or reducing costs. In fact, it serves as a model for corporate attitude that goes beyond the whole team approach that has permeated corporate project work for so many years.

Two attributes need to be present in order for any quality control program to work. First, that program cannot be isolated or defined as a function that occurs in the plant alone, or in the office, department, or subsidiary. It has to be a working philosophy that applies from the boardroom to the mail room; everyone can participate in an overall quality control approach to corporate success. In fact, the real success stories in the corporate world have been able to demonstrate effective, corporate-wide quality ideals.

1

The second attribute is that "quality" itself cannot be applied only to one portion of the corporate environment. Quality control has its root in manufacturing, where it was applied to develop ways to reduce defects, increase productivity, and ensure on-time delivery of goods. Today, quality control is just as important in the service sector, and quality control measures can be used effectively by applying the lessons learned in the manufacturing industries. Six Sigma is a quality control approach that can and should be applied to all interactions: with customers, vendors, other employees, between management and departments, within manufacturing or production departments, and even between corporations and regulatory agencies.

In other words, the idea of quality control is not simply a method by which management tries to cut costs, squeeze out more units of production, or give employees a voice on an internal team. While all of those benefits accrue from a quality control program, they are among the *results* of a more universally applied and systematic point of view. A traditional organization has boards and officers at the top, operational leadership, and then managers and employees far down the line. The more complex the organizational chain of command, the more difficult it becomes to achieve any meaningful or effective quality control. It becomes easy for a manager to recognize a problem elsewhere, but to shrug it off. "It's not my problem" is the default position.

With the universal approach to quality, we recognize something that is both obvious and all-important. Any problem within the company is a shared responsibility because, ultimately, defects (whether related to product or service, customer service, communication, or compliance) are going to affect the corporation and all of its employees, officers, and stockholders. In the long term, dynamically organized and effectively managed corporations are going to succeed, and segmented, inert, disorganized, bureaucratic, and ineffective corporations are going to lose customer base. As markets decline, those companies also experience declines in vendor relations, employee morale, and internal communication.

Quality, for all its mundane attributes, can be far more than the trite concept that so many have come to view with well-deserved cynicism. If quality control is only an expression used to describe management's way of dealing with cost overruns, it has no significance beyond that limited application. A quality control program that demands better results without involving the worker in the broader corporate-wide idea, can be of limited value alone. For those corporations that prefer demanding higher quality without creating a sense of real teamwork, the opportunities are going to be missed. Ultimately, their competitors—who recognize the opportunities to create very effective and dynamic quality programs—are going to take market share away.

Six Sigma is an effective approach to a broad-based quality control program. It is far more than the traditional approach, in which internal teams are created to reduce production defects, solve problems within one department, and address problems in isolation. Six Sigma is more than a quality control program with another name; it is a quality-based system for reorganizing the entire approach to work in every aspect: productivity, communication, involvement at every level, and external service.

Because Six Sigma and its guidelines improve performance and communication on many levels, it changes not only the outcome (service, production, or communication) but affects the very way that we communicate with each other and with customers and vendors. Programs may begin with focus on a single problem, such as errors in customer deliveries or the inability to keep products in inventory, but the solutions are not isolated. If a vice president responds to a problem by insisting that it be fixed at the departmental level—and without examining its broader implications—an opportunity is lost. If that same vice president involves the entire corporation in a study of how and why such problems evolve, they will find more permanent solutions. This does not mean a complex, expensive analysis has to be used; rather, Six Sigma is designed for rapid, simple problem solving that involves all levels and all contacts (employee, customer, vendor).

This book is designed to show, step by step, how Six Sigma works and how it can be used most effectively. Whether you are an executive or manager trying to change your approach to problem solving, or an employee in a corporation with a Six Sigma program, this book is structured to lead you through each step of the process. It includes definitions in margins, placed at the point of discussion. This enables you to master the terminology as you read along. We use many examples, checklists, and graphics to further help you in developing a working knowledge of Six Sigma.

If we hope to become more effective in production, service, and communication, we need not only to improve our internal approach; we also need to help our fellow employees, supervisors, and managers to move along the same path. Effectiveness on every level is the goal and purpose to Six Sigma. The broad-based quality ideal—an appreciation of what is needed to strive for perfection— requires that everyone in the company understands its importance and their part in achieving it.

Chapter

The Meaning of Six Sigma

Many years ago at Fisherman's Wharf in San Francisco, I saw a fisherman sewing up holes in his net. The net was quite large and he had lain it out over a wide expanse of the dock. I watched him for quite some time, noticing that he paid careful attention to even the smallest tear, methodically repairing each one in turn. When he took a break I walked over to him. "Why do you have to fix all the tears, even the little ones?" I asked him. He explained, "It only takes one small tear for all of the fish to escape."

Perfection—impossible to achieve completely and all of the time—is a goal worth keeping in mind. If we set our sights any lower, we deserve what we get. If we settle for 80 percent or 70 percent, we can never expect to reach 95 percent or 98 percent. As the old fisherman explained, even the smallest imperfection affects the entire effort. A small tear in the net becomes a bigger tear and the fish escape as the net is pulled in. The corporate world works in the same way. What might seem a minor imperfection or a flaw in a remote department affects you and your product or service. The solution: We have to find all the tears and repair them, methodically and completely. Yes, new tears will appear in the net, but we cannot shrug and explain, "We found most of them." We also cannot just shrug and say, "It's not my job." Perfection is not a requirement, but it is a goal worth setting. We can then compare our outcomes to the goal, seeing improvement and measuring it against that goal.

THE ORIGINS OF SIX SIGMA

Sigma is the letter in the Greek alphabet used to denote standard deviation, a statistical measurement of variation, the exceptions to expected outcomes. *Standard deviation* can be thought of as a comparison between expected results or outcomes in a group of operations, versus those that fail.

The measurement of standard deviation shows us that rates of defects, or exceptions, are measurable. *Six Sigma* is the definition of outcomes as close as possible to perfection. With six standard deviations, we arrive at 3.4 defects per million opportunities, or 99.9997 percent. This would mean that at Six Sigma, an airline would lose only three pieces of luggage for every one million that it handles; or that the phone company would have only three unhappy customers out of every one million who use the phone that day. The *purpose* in evaluating defects is not to eliminate them entirely, but to strive for improvement to the highest possible level that we can achieve.

Key Point We evaluate defects to improve overall performance, knowing that eliminating them completely is unrealistic.

We know that trying to achieve Six Sigma would be impractical on a consistent basis; so while it is a desirable goal, it presents a model against which we can measure our performance. So rather than setting the unrealistic goal of achieving perfection, we can observe (1) our current Sigma level and (2) improvement in that level as changes are made.

Table 1.1 presents an abbreviated summary of Sigma level, defects per million, and yield, or success rate of the outcomes.

You can identify your level of Sigma performance and then compare it to the chart. This is where the bene-

sigma
the level of variation compared to an average; the Greek letter, σ used by statisticians to denote standard deviation.

standard deviation
the degree of exception, or variation from the average, in a group of outcomes, used to describe exceptions to an expected result.

Six Sigma
a measurement denoting near perfection, representing six standard deviations or 3.4 million defects per million operations; the ideal against which actual performance is measured.

TABLE 1.1 Sigma Table		
Sigma	Defects per Million	Yield
6.0	3.4	99.9997%
5.0	233.0	99.977
4.0	6,210.0	99.379
3.0	66,807.0	93.32
2.5	158,655.0	84.1
2.0	308,538.0	69.1
1.5	500,000.0	50.0
1.4	539,828.0	46.0
1.3	579,260.0	42.1
1.2	617,911.0	38.2
1.1	655,422.0	34.5
1.0	691,462.0	30.9
0.5	841,345.0	15.9
0.0	933,193.0	6.7

fits of Six Sigma are realized. By comparing your outcomes to the ideal outcome of Six Sigma, you can quantify quality itself.

Example: Your department performed 535 specific operations last month. Of these, 43 were defective (they fell outside the acceptable range of outcomes). This means that 492 of the operations were successful. The yield was:

$$492 \div 535 = 91.9\%$$

Referring to Table 1.1, we discover that this outcome represents Sigma somewhere between 2.5 and 3. If you were able to reduce the number of defects by half, ending up with 21, your acceptable outcomes would then grow to 514 out of 535 operations, and your yield would increase as well:

$$514 \div 535 = 96.1\%$$

Now the Sigma is between 3 and 4, a significant improvement. Of course, if you cut defects in half, you are going to know your outcomes have improved, so what purpose does Six Sigma provide beyond the obvious scorekeeping? As the preceding example demonstrates, improvement in quality can be specifically measured. In practice, you may be dealing with a much greater volume of outcomes, and the incremental rate of success is likely to be smaller than that shown in the example; and Six Sigma is far more than a measuring system. It is a way of doing things, a change in cultural attitude that is designed to create a company-wide team in practical terms. As far as the scorekeeping aspects of Six Sigma go, if you begin with an assumption that a change in procedures will produce an expected change in outcomes, you can then compare actual to projected results to judge the success of your work.

Key Point What makes Six Sigma different from most other quality control programs? It is more than just a way to improve performance; it is a method for changing the corporate culture, from top to bottom.

An "operation" can be any function you perform—delivery of goods, telephone contact, balancing accounts, or executing a repair, for example. Any operation is measurable in Sigma terms. The desired outcome represents satisfaction of the customer's expectation, and any time that expectation is not met, the outcome is defective.

While measuring results is a crucial part of the process, you will be more concerned with how Six Sigma is applied and what role you and other employees will perform within that process. So the idea of Six Sigma is much more than the latest approach to quality control; it represents a change in philosophy that affects everyone. It is designed to bring everyone into a single team with the same overall goals. So many corporate employees—especially in large organizations—have a sense of isolation or view their relatively small department as a realm unto itself. Six Sigma encompasses the entire corporation as a single team and is aimed at removing that sense of isolation.

The concept of Six Sigma began at Motorola in the 1980s. An engineer named Mikel Harry began analyzing variation in outcomes in the company's internal procedures, and realized that by measuring variation it would be possible to improve working systems. However, whereas other quality systems were designed at only measuring performance, the Six Sigma approach that grew from Harry's original ideas was different. The procedures were aimed at taking action to change procedures so that overall performance could be improved permanently— and at every level within the company.

Within a few years, the same idea had taken root at General Electric and AlliedSignal. GE decided in 1995 to implement Six Sigma throughout the entire organization. CEO Jack Welch led the company through this implementation, and many divisions of GE experienced impressive improvements in quality during those years. Estimates are that cost savings from Six Sigma application exceeded $320 million within the first two years, and more than $1 billion by 1999.[1]

Key Point Cost savings are an important aspect of quality control, but they are only *one* aspect; a permanent, effective, and rewarding quality program requires more work.

So many quality programs have been devised, named, and put into effect over many years. Most fail after a while because employees lose faith in those programs. It becomes obvious to employees that "quality control" really represents management's attempt to cut costs and expenses and get more work from its labor force. In other words, the program applies to the worker but there is no change in management itself. If the final result of a quality program is to achieve increased efficiency, and that results in layoffs, who benefits? With Six Sigma, everyone is involved and everyone is expected to change (for the better) as part of one overall team. The purpose is not assigned to the rank and file, but is shared from top to bottom.

BUSINESS PROCESS MANAGEMENT (BPM) AS A STARTING POINT

Like all other specialized processes, Six Sigma involves the use of a series of specialized terms. They have specific meaning and are important in distinguishing the roles that people play in executing the successful Six Sigma procedure.

The concept of Six Sigma begins with a process model and its implementation is called *Business Process Management (BPM)*. Using the BPM model allows us to understand how work evolves and to move *through* the organization from input to output.

> **BPM (Business Process Management)** an approach to work based on a model (Business Process Model) describing how work moves from step to step through the organization.

To visualize how BPM helps us to (1) design, (2) communicate, and (3) improve systems, we use a flowchart. Those who grew up in the computer age are accustomed to seeing flowcharts that move from top to bottom. We have come to think of work flow in similar terms; but in practice, we can better express the workings of a procedure when we express work flow from left to right. This is not merely the mincing of words or the moving of a vertical flowchart to a horizontal one. In fact, the horizontal BMP model is a powerful tool for identifying likely problem areas within processes and then for taking steps to decrease defects.

The design of the basic model horizontal flowchart is shown in Figure 1.1.

Note that there appear to be three horizontal levels in the process area of this illustration. These represent de-

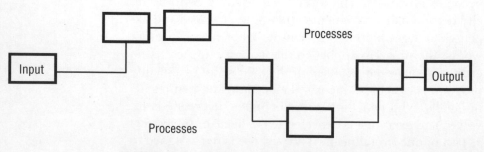

FIGURE 1.1 Model horizontal flowchart.

partments, individuals, or other sub-teams that perform specific functions. Because the exact mix of responsibility is likely to vary from one process to another, these may be described as areas of responsibility.

A timeline can be added along the bottom, if desired, to indicate how timing comes into play in the process. Additionally, any reports or other generated work documents can be identified with drop-down boxes. This ties the interim output to the area of responsibility, point in the process, and timing of the task.

Key Point The horizontal flowchart is not just a passive work flow summary; it is a working document used for identifying the steps in a process and, most significantly, for highlighting the likely places where variances, or defects, are most likely to occur.

In determining how to best improve quality, we have to first ensure that work flow is logical and complete. The horizontal flowchart used for BPM enables us to examine each step along the way to make sure we understand time requirements, steps and sequence, and specific responsibility. These include determining what has to be received in order to execute a step, and what has to be passed on for the next step. This is a methodical and precise method, both for defining work flow and finding likely variables—where defects or failures are likely to occur. Figure 1.2 highlights these points in the process.

In the figure, we have identified exact steps in the process where we believe variances are most likely to occur, or where defects are likely to be generated. These points are identified as black rectangles. The assumption in a process involving multiple areas of responsibility is that the likely variance points are strongest when processes move from one area to another. As long as a process is confined to a single area of responsibility, its steps can be managed by a limited number of supervisors or managers. When more than one area of responsibility comes into play, we can place emphasis on the points where a step is completed and the process then moves elsewhere. This is where problems are most likely to arise.

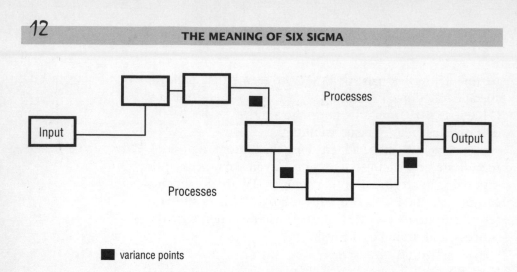

FIGURE 1.2   Model horizontal flowchart with variance points.

These include a failure to act in a timely manner, processing with incomplete data, interpretations containing errors, and similar, common variances.

We further expand the horizontal flowchart to identify both a timeline and interim documents generated throughout the process. This is shown in Figure 1.3.

In this expanded version of the horizontal flowchart, we have a complete picture: Areas of responsibility, process flow from one step to another (including changes between areas of responsibility), likely variance and defect points, a timeline, and interim and final reports.

Understanding the essential importance of BPM is a starting point in Six Sigma. For example, if you have a process riddled with defects, the best way to identify the problem—as a starting point—is to prepare the horizontal flowchart. By methodically speaking with each person, department, or team involved in the process, we can put together a complete picture of how it works and how it *should* work. This highlights variance points leading to identification of likely defect points so that appropriate changes can be made. This is how the Sigma level is effectively raised—by focusing on variance points and enforcing procedures where those occur.

The flowchart approach to defining processes can be used effectively for improving existing procedures, mak-

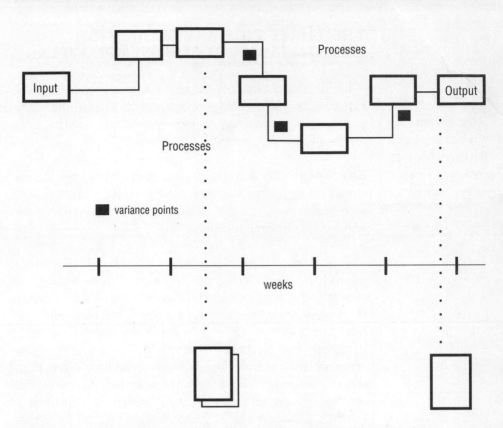

FIGURE 1.3 Model horizontal flowchart with variance points, timeline, and documents.

ing process changes, merging two or more procedures, or developing new procedures. The flowchart also serves as an excellent training tool. It provides new employees with a view in the context of their roles in a larger procedure, as well as providing steps in sequence. The flowchart identifies each element within the process from beginning to end so that everyone involved can view not only their role, but the roles of others as well. When accompanied with the more traditional procedural documentation, this visualized form of process flow is a powerful internal quality control and training tool. A more detailed example of the horizontal flowchart and its practical application—both as a Six Sigma tool and an internal document—is provided in Chapter 6.

THE THREE PRIMARY ELEMENTS: CUSTOMERS, PROCESSES, EMPLOYEES

With Six Sigma, the purpose of the whole exercise is to locate defects, identify ways to prevent them, and make improvements permanent. A *defect* is any outcome that does not satisfy the needs of the "customer."

> **defect**
> any outcome that falls short of the customer's needs or expectations.

Key Point In defining a customer, many people are surprised to realize that everyone is in the customer service business—even the clerk who never gets out of the windowless basement office.

You may notice that we have placed quotations around the word "customer." This was done for a good reason: We want to expand the definition of this word. In the widely understood sense, a customer is someone who buys our goods or services. It is usually someone outside the company—a consumer, another company, or the government, for example. In Six Sigma, you may serve a different customer. Those in nonmarketing environments are often described as people who "never see a customer," but this is not an accurate assumption. We all have customers. As a basic definition of a job, we provide something of value to someone else. So your customer may be another department or a group of employees within your own company.

The accounting department usually has little or no contact outside the company. However, it prepares budgets, reports, and payroll checks for a wide variety of departments and people. If someone does not receive their paycheck on the day expected, it means there is a defect in the process within the payroll accounting department. There is little doubt that the department will hear from its "customer" very quickly.

A shipping and receiving department deals with delivery services, the post office, or a trucking company, and is responsible for making sure that any goods to be received or delivered are expedited in a timely manner. If a package does not show up on either end or is delivered to the wrong address, or the contents are broken in transit, those outcomes have failed to meet the needs of the customer. That customer could be a buyer, a vendor, a clerk in the mail room, or the CEO. We cannot limit the definition of "customer" only to those who buy what our company sells; large numbers of employees deal with other types of customers.

Example: The accounts payable department is responsible for making timely payments to vendors. A marketing employee has promised payment to a valued vendor by the 15th of the month. This promise was mentioned in paperwork forwarded to accounts payable, with a note explaining that the items being purchased were essential for a marketing presentation. The vendor would not make delivery until payment was received. The accounts payable department scheduled payment for the 18th, not realizing that the deadline of the 15th was critical.

In this example, a defect occurred due to a collapse in communication. The flaw in procedure is shared by the marketing employee who did not follow up to ensure that the importance of the timing was comprehended. The accounts payable department assigned a payment date without checking the paperwork thoroughly. This type of failure is typical when process flows from one department to another. The defect cannot be blamed or assigned, because in each case, both sides were involved, and both sides failed to take quality control steps to make sure the defect did not occur. The marketing employee is aware of the customer who requires payment by a specific date, a requisite for timely delivery. The accounts payable employee, however, has not been made aware of his or her customer's needs, because that customer (the marketing employee) did not communicate well enough to ensure a smooth process.

Key Point For the purpose of identifying quality requirements, we need to first understand the customer's requirements and expectations.

It is not difficult to see how a relatively simply change in procedure could eliminate virtually all defects in this type of transaction. If anyone requesting payment were to institute a follow-up procedure, it would improve communication at the source (assuming they followed the procedure, of course). If accounts payable were to check paperwork and then follow up to eliminate any uncertainty, it would also do away with the majority of defective outcomes. This doubled-up procedure would reduce the chances for defects. So the marketing department is expected to follow up and ensure timely payment, and accounts payable is supposed to make sure it knows when payments are to be made. If *either* one follows their procedure, a potential defect will be avoided. The steps to nearly foolproof procedures are often simple, and the resulting changes can be dramatic as well. With human error added into the equation, some defects are going to occur. However, by tracking the flaw, we can again bolster up the procedures so that processes run far more smoothly, and so that human error can be managed and outcomes moved up to a higher Sigma.

Customers, processes, and employees are the three primary elements in operating within the Six Sigma quality control environment. The customer (an end customer in the traditional definition or another department or person in the broader definition) depends on a specific employee or department to operate within the process and to deliver the needed and expected outcome. In this case, the outcome was the *timely* payment. A late payment is a defect. In the accounts payable environment, a *timely* payment may be assumed to be 30 days unless otherwise indicated—remembering, however, that assumptions may themselves lead to defects. So if we are to assume that it is universally understood that the 30-day cycle is in operation unless otherwise specified, we have a starting point. The default presumption is in operation unless someone reads instructions on a check requisition, receives a telephone call, or—lacking any specific information—makes a telephone call to check whether the 30-day default is acceptable.

The interaction between customers, processes, and

employees is complex. Every situation is different, so every definition of a defect is different as well. The accounts payable department might wish to define defects as "late" payments, meaning a payment beyond 30 days. So any request for a check to be issued prior to 30 days is an exception. By this definition, the payment in the example would not be called a defect as long as it was made within the 30-day default period. The problem here is that from the marketing department's point of view, expedited payment is needed and if it is not made, there is a defect. One goal of Six Sigma is to reconcile these different definitions of "defects" from two sides involved in the same process.

Key Point   Definition of a customer's requirements may not be the same on both sides of the transaction; we need to come to an agreement about what those requirements are before we can expect to fix or avoid problems.

This demonstrates how an effective quality control system has to go beyond the traditional way that departments and people work with one another. If the definition of a defect is going to be made secondary to an unrealistic definition, then the quality control program is destined to fail. The departmental attitude—"It's not my problem"—has to be replaced with a broader view. If a person chooses to believe that the world is flat, the potential dangers of travel are not an issue as long as that person never leaves home. However, as long as that individual continues to hold onto the flat-world belief, he or she will be of little value if the task at hand is to map out an expedition to distant lands.

Perhaps the accounts payable department is being asked to travel to distant lands and challenge its own assumptions. Under Six Sigma, the department would acknowledge that the assumption based on a 30-day timetable is unrealistic in many instances; they cannot expect the world to conform to the view most convenient to them: universal application of a payment cycle to *all* instances where checks are to be issued. While many payments conform to that model, the nature of accounts payable is to make a variety of accommodations for its customers (including vendors, other departments, and their fellow employees). These accommodations include the flexibility to cut a check immediately or to accept a variety of deadline terms as part of the payment. In this department, a *defect* results from a flawed assumption. So the very method of processing has to be examined and modified. Instead of viewing a 30-day payment term as the default position, the department needs to begin the process with the question "When is the payment due?" If most payments are due within 30 days, they can be managed according to that procedure; but if some other terms apply, the process has to be set up to manage it. Exceptions can be processed smoothly as long as the system looks for them. It is invariably a mistake to allow the rigid presumptions of a process to overrule the exceptions in the interest of more efficient (but flawed) processes.

That process itself is a primary element in the customer-process-employee interaction, and it has to work with the customers and employees. While this requirement may seem obvious, it is not always put into practice. When the process sets the rules and customers or employees have to conform to it, defects have to be expected. For example, imagine the outcome if a vendor agreed to deliver on condition that payment arrives by the 15th, and the marketing employee responded, "I cannot promise payment until 30 days from now."

You would expect the vendor to refuse to ship, or to have to change the terms to accommodate the marketing employee. These types of unsatisfactory outcomes take place every day. In the case of the vendor and marketing employee, the goods might be delivered, but the vendor's opinion of the company declines. So the defect in this case would be invisible because the goods get delivered— but the goodwill loss, perhaps a significant one, is not visible to anyone observing the process. Some may even shrug it off, observing that the vendor needs the account more than the company needs the vendor, so he or she has to change the fast-payment procedure, "or we will use someone else."

Key Point We should be concerned about losing good-will with our customers, whether they are found outside the company or in the department down the hall.

Vendor service, a variation of customer service, is often ignored or overlooked in the corporate environment that operates based on process alone. If you are not aware of quality control in all of its aspects, then the processes dominate the interaction. That vendor, who is a customer in every sense, will suffer from the defect. It may be that the goods the vendor is supplying have to be purchased elsewhere to be processed, so the vendor has to invest a large sum of money. This would explain why fast payment is essential, and a reasonable requirement as well. The accounts payable rule that payments go out "net 30" is not always fair or realistic. Flexibility gives you the edge. Your market consists of a range of different customers, and the more you are able to provide a responsive outcome free of defects, the higher the quality of your product.

ADDITIONAL ELEMENTS: SUBCONTRACTORS AND REGULATORS

Vendors and other employees or departments are customers in the quality control environment. The definition of customers is not limited to these, either. You also serve the needs of subcontractors and regulators, who also are your customers.

A "subcontractor" may be another department, an outside provider, or another operating unit within your organization. It is an error to view the subcontractor as a noncustomer. In fact, once you begin looking for customers and treating all contacts as customer service opportunities, the quality in your department or area of responsibility is likely to rise dramatically. As part of the broader operating philosophy of Six Sigma, customer service is not limited to those who buy something from us. We are surrounded by customers, each with a variety of expectations. Whether our product is a report, a check, an answer to a question, or a package, we are providers to many, and they are our customers. If those outsiders also adopt the attitude that in some respects, you are their customer, the whole process takes on a new face and quality control works throughout the organization—with fewer defects.

We mention regulators in the same section with subcontractors for a good reason. The usual attitude toward regulators deserves a fresh look. Traditionally, we view regulation as an imposition from the outside, and if we did not have to submit, we would not. It provides nothing productive or valuable. Regulation is adversarial, an intrusion.

In the broader view, the regulatory environment can be viewed as a customer as well. Listed companies, for example, have to deal with stock exchange listing standards, federal and state reporting and disclosure requirements, and an independent audit. All of these routines provide something of value. Stockholders would not invest with any confidence if regulators did not examine the books of the corporation. The independent auditor as a service provider relates to the corporation as its customer or client. At the same time, departments within the company provide answers to questions, documents and files, and process suggestions to auditors and to regulators, so in that respect, some internal departments (such as financial reporting and accounting departments and internal auditing) may view regulatory agencies as "customers." If it is their responsibility to comply with the needs of an auditing firm or a federal or state regulator, then those agencies are, indeed, the department's customers.

Key Point　The idea of applying customer service to a regulator is contrary to popular thinking, but it makes sense. And it is also good business practice.

While the popular view of regulators is negative, you may view the provider-to-customer approach to working within this environment, thus improving performance. If your job includes compliance with a regulatory agency, taking the customer service approach is appropriate. To the extent that you provide accurate, timely, and useful information, you improve your performance. Even without viewing a regulatory agency as a "customer" per se, it remains a valid point that your performance should be as excellent as possible. When it comes to regulators, we may remind ourselves that we do not have to like the customer to provide good customer service. You may view regulation as a necessary evil and an inconvenience—just as a busy retail clerk will view a customer with many questions. That clerk performs the task with excellent service by remaining courteous and responsive, even when they would rather usher everyone out and lock the doors.

THE PARTICIPANTS IN SIX SIGMA

Whether you like your customer or not, your customer service system can and should be as defect free as possible—even if only to make your job easier. Under a Six Sigma program, members of your organization are assigned specific roles to play, each with a title. This highly structured format is necessary in order to implement Six Sigma throughout the organization, because the chain of command in your company will not necessarily apply in the Six Sigma environment. For the quality control program to work well, the reporting chain has to be suspended. There are seven specific responsibilities or "role areas" in the Six Sigma program. These are:

leadership council
the team or committee that defines the specific goals of a Six Sigma process, the provider of goals to be met by the team.

1. *Leadership.* A leadership team or council defines the goals and objectives in the Six Sigma process. Just as a corporate leader sets a tone and course to achieve an objective, the Six Sigma council sets out the goals to be met by the team. A checklist of some areas the council would undertake as responsibilities is shown in Table 1.2.

By following this list, the leadership council becomes results oriented. You expect any leader to demand and expect the desired outcome, in terms of quality, deadline and problem solving. Six Sigma can work only when results are meaningful and improve overall customer service. This usually will mean higher customer satisfaction due to reduced incidence of defects.

TABLE 1.2 Checklist, Leadership Council Responsibilities

Responsibility	Description of Duties
1. Define the purpose of the Six Sigma Program	Definition is the key to initiating any project; the council begins by identifying the reasons for undertaking a specific activity.
2. Explain how the result is going to benefit the customer	Every Six Sigma program is aimed at meeting the needs of the customer; improving performance; and reducing the incidence of defects. The program needs to be structured in these terms.
3. Set a schedule for work and interim deadlines	The project is broken down into logical sequence and phases, each with deadlines for (1) review, (2) change, and (3) final version.
4. Develop a means for review and oversight	As the project progresses, work is monitored to ensure it is on track and properly focused. This phase also ensures that each team member is executing responsibilities as expected.
5. Support team members and defend established positions	The real leadership in Six Sigma is demonstrated by how well the council defends the process. Enthusiastic adherence to Six Sigma principles ensures that the team will remain cohesive.

sponsor
the problem solver within a Six Sigma project, usually a manager who implements the orders passed down by the council; often the process owner, or person who is ultimately responsible for completing a process.

2. *Sponsor.* The individual in the sponsor role acts as a problem solver for the ongoing Six Sigma project. Usually a senior manager within the company, the sponsor implements the leadership council's orders and smoothes out any conflicts that arise. The sponsor often has a keen sense of the need for a Six Sigma process because he or she will end up managing the process after the team has revamped it. The sponsor's responsibilities are listed in Table 1.3.

3. *Implementation leader or director.* The implementation leader is responsible for overseeing the entire Six Sigma effort for a team (or group of teams). He or she supports the leadership team or council by ensuring that their mandate is implemented; recommends people for important roles on a Six Sigma team, either from within the company or from outside resources; ensuring success

TABLE 1.3 Checklist, Sponsor Responsibilities	
Responsibility	*Description of Duties*
1. Maintain focus on the goals defined by the leadership	The sponsor ensures that team members keep the ultimate goal in mind and keep focused toward it.
2. Supervise and train team members as needed	The sponsor acts as supervisor, making sure that team members understand their tasks and know how to complete them. When extra training or support is needed, the sponsor provides it.
3. Act as representative of the team with the leadership	As work progresses, the sponsor represents the team and, when necessary, defends them or speaks for them as representative.
4. Find and manage needed project resources	Six Sigma work is not always performed within a single area or department. The sponsor acts as go-between when help is needed between departments or operating units.
5. Mediate any conflicts or disagreements within the team or with outside areas	Individuals within one team may find themselves in conflict with one another; or the work of the team might be in conflict with another team. The sponsor is a coordinator, responsible for solving this problem.

of the implementation plan and solving problems as they arise; training as needed; and assisting sponsors in motivating the team.

4. *Coach.* The term coach implies a trainer or guide. In the Six Sigma team, the coach serves as an expert or consultant to the team and its members. Duties include working as go-between for sponsor and leadership; scheduling the work of the team; identifying and defining desired results of the project; mediating disagreements, conflicts, and resistance to the program; and identifying success as it occurs.

5. *Team leader.* The day-to-day work of the Six Sigma team is managed by the team leader. Responsibilities include communication with the sponsor in defining project goals and rationale; picking and assisting team members and other resources; keeping the project on

implementation leader
the person responsible for supervising the Six Sigma team effort, who supports the leadership council by ensuring that the work of the team is completed in the desired manner.

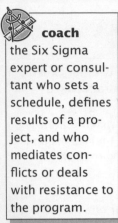

coach
the Six Sigma expert or consultant who sets a schedule, defines results of a project, and who mediates conflicts or deals with resistance to the program.

team leader
the individual responsible for overseeing the work of the team, and for acting as go-between with the sponsor and the team members; the person who manages the schedule.

team member
an employee who works on a Six Sigma project, given specific duties within a project, and deadlines to meet in reaching specific project goals.

schedule; and keeping track of steps in the process as they are completed.

6. *Team member.* A team can have a number of definitions within the organization. It often refers to a group of people working together from different units or departments. The team members execute specific Six Sigma assignments and work with other members of the team within a defined project schedule, to reach specifically identified goals.

7. *Process owner.* The process owner ends up with an improved procedure, or is assigned responsibility for executing processes newly designed by the team.

It may seem that there are an unnecessarily large number of layers in the Six Sigma process. Why the formality? First, we need to clarify that these rules represent a maximum number of tiers in a Six Sigma process, but they are not all required. Some may be combined and executed by the same person. In a very complex project involving many different departments and requiring a long time for completion, a highly structured procedure—with frequent review, strict oversight, and well-defined responsibilities—is desirable. In a shorter-term project involving only one or two departments, the structure of the Six Sigma organization can be more abbreviated.

Key Point   The multiple layers and titles in a Six Sigma operation often can be reduced or combined. The formalized structure allows for flexibility, so that projects of all sizes can be managed appropriately within the Six Sigma approach.

The organization of the overall Six Sigma system is summarized in Figure 1.4.

PARTICIPANT WITHIN SIX SIGMA

Many labels have evolved over the years that Six Sigma has been in use. These labels originated at founding com-

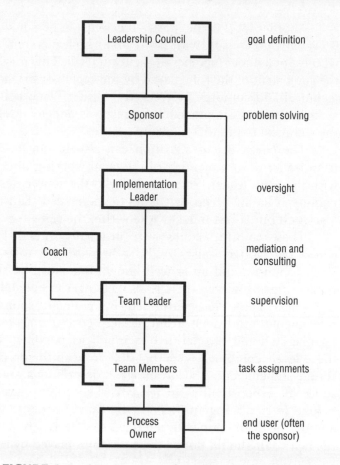

FIGURE 1.4 Organization of the Six Sigma program.

> **process owner**
> the individual who takes on responsibility for a process after a Six Sigma team has completed its work.

pany Motorola, but the definitions have been extended by other users since then.

The assignment of belt colors to various roles is derived from the obvious source, martial arts. At the top of the achievement level in karate, for example, is the *Black Belt*. The person possessing this belt has achieved the highest skill level and is an experienced expert in various techniques. As applied to the Six Sigma program, the individual designated as a Black Belt will have completed a thorough internal training program and have experienced work on several projects. The black belt holder is usually given the role of team leader, the person who is responsible for execution and scheduling.

> **Black Belt**
> An experienced participant in the Six Sigma process, usually given the role of team leader, who is responsible for ensuring that the benefits of Six Sigma projects are realized.

Master Black Belt a consultant (sometimes the coach) available to the Six Sigma team to resolve technical issues or to answer questions.

Green Belt the sponsor or a key team member with a degree of experience above the average team member, or who plays a key role in helping the sponsor manage the scheduling and assignments within a project.

Another level is the *Master Black Belt*, a person who is available to consult with the team or its leadership but who is not a direct member of the team itself. This may be the equivalent of the role played by the coach; or for more technical and complex projects, the Master Black Belt is available to answer procedural questions and to resolve the technical issues that come up.

The *Green Belt* designation can also belong to the team leader or to a member of the team working directly with the team leader. Referring back to the source designations, a karate green belt is less experienced than the black belt but is cast in a key role within the team.

These colorful names were originally intended to add a descriptive sense to the otherwise dry roles of leader, sponsor, and other well-known but overused corporate titles. However, there is also a danger in overdefining roles. The roles performed by council, sponsor, implementation leader, team leader, coach, and team members should be clarified as much as possible; and those levels combined when possible to keep the process simple and efficient. The advantage of describing a role or series of responsibilities in terms of belt colors may be helpful in exhibiting an individual's team experience and ability. The distinction between the actual designation and the belt color should not confuse the roles played by each participant on the team.

Key Point   The belt names are one tool for defining levels of expertise and experience. They do not change or replace the organizational roles in the Six Sigma process.

GOALS OF THE PROGRAM

In any undertaking that is going to place demands on time, budgets, and other resources, we need to begin with a definition of the perceived benefits we hope to derive. In the case of a corporate-wide Six Sigma program, the intention is to change the entire corporate culture for the better.

Beginning with the traditional customer—the receiver or products or services that we provide—it is apparent that the best internal systems cannot be developed in isolation. In some respects, we learn from our mistakes so that an exceptional system is the result of trial and error. However, such a system may also be developed by listening to the customer. If customer satisfaction is the primary focus of a Six Sigma program, we cannot ignore the customer's expectations, because that set of expectations defines quality and enables us to spot defects. The questions that every corporate leader and employee should be asking are based on acknowledging that the customer *defines* quality itself. As GE's former CEO explained:

The best Six Sigma projects begin not inside the business but outside it, focused on answering the question, How can we make the customer more competitive? What is critical to the customer's success?[2]

Customer satisfaction is the essential and defining concern for all quality programs. If we also extend that definition so that *all* of us deal with a "customer" in some manner, then the smart theories of improved customer relations can be applied across the entire organization. One of the beliefs that harms morale among nonmarketing employees is the polarizing observation that they never see or speak to a customer. So an elite subculture arises, in which marketing employees bring in the profits while nonmarketing people merely shuffle paper. This is one of the most damaging themes seen in corporations, and it is most pronounced in companies involved with marketing directly to customers.

Key Point The belief that there are two kinds of employees—those who see customers and those who do not—is damaging to morale and impedes the development of a quality control system. Everyone has a customer, and once this is recognized, the real job of creating a company-wide team can begin.

So as a goal, it is not enough to define the program as aimed toward improving customer service; it should also extend that definition so that everyone, even those merely shuffling papers, can adopt the same attitude focused on improved customer service. This brings us to a second goal of any quality control program: employee involvement. As a member of a department, an employee is likely to be expected to focus very narrowly on specific functions, deadlines, and procedures. These processes are often best performed in an isolated manner, while a supervisor or manager worries about interaction with other departments or with management. Depending on the type of department, the limitation of processes often makes sense. When it comes to a broader involvement in and participation in quality control, that same employee is given a different type of incentive. This ownership over processes—derived from developing improved, more creative, more efficient, or more profitable methodology—is satisfying and rewarding and may give the employee a sense of real participation. This satisfaction may be lacking in the departmental routines and attendant deadlines. So quality participation can do a lot to improve employee morale. Allowing people to define how processes can be improved is perhaps the single most important step a company can take to improve morale among its employees.

In defining customers, we may also look at employees in that light. In many respects, the employee is the "customer" of the department supervisor or manager, the vice president, and the CEO. Management has a responsibility to the company's employees and, if we are to include vendors as "customers," we should certainly extend the same status to employees—and for good reason. If we exclude the employee from the broad definition of "customer," then we cannot expect that employee to respond to improved internal processes that come from Six Sigma projects. Any project that improves service to customers or vendors has to also improve the quality of corporate life for employees. Positive change invariably has that effect, but we have to be aware that we need to change a cultural attitude. Six Sigma participation is intended to help employees—whether marketing or administrative—to move beyond the demoralizing characterization of some employees as having no customer contact.

Finally, we expect Six Sigma to work universally. So the same redefined "customer" embraces the subcontractor and even the regulator. A subcontractor may be a company that works within the corporate structure without being a part of the formal reporting chain, such as a consulting firm, for example. And while applying a standard of customer service to those agencies within the regulatory environment may seem odd, it makes perfect sense. In defining the types of defects we expect to see when dealing with the regulatory customer, we conclude that improved quality is beneficial to everyone.

For example, a regulator may be interested in ensuring that disclosures are made properly to investors. (This would apply to federal and state securities agencies and to stock exchanges for companies that are publicly listed.) So a department or team whose task is to ensure compliance with the disclosure rules should be interested in discovering internal defects; identifying their causes; and making recommendations to fix the root problems. This is the ultimate outcome at any rate, although the requirement often is imposed by the agency at the conclusion of an audit. It makes more sense to look for those problems and fix them internally as a response to the requirements of the customer—in this case a regulator.

Six Sigma truly does apply over the whole spectrum of the organization, not only because it is intended to create a universal team, but also because it simply makes sense. Quality control defined as a method for cutting costs only, without the complete involvement of management, may be sold as a means for improving morale. But the failure of such programs is due to the real effect they have always had: reducing employee morale. Once we address every problem from the customer's point of view, we begin to see how and why corporate-wide quality is the most sensible system. This is the subject of the next chapter.

Chapter 2

The Customer's Point of View

I was in one of the big Sears stores during the time the company was trying to offer financial services along with retail. I overheard a lady interrupting a Dean Witter representative who was in the middle of a discussion with a customer. She asked, "Where is the boys' underwear department?" The expression on the broker's face revealed the problem. Everyone within earshot realized suddenly what the problem was: People were uncomfortable with a single outlet offering everything. The joke about Sears became "It is the store where you can buy stocks, socks, and jocks."

Is it enough to provide excellent *service* to your customer? Can exceptional service or too much attention become irritating? If "service" exceeds what a customer wants, perhaps we need to go back to the drawing board and look at our definitions once again.

Six Sigma is intended not only to continually improve quality. Of course, that is going to be a primary aim, but we cannot always use the manufacturing model of units of production and degrees of defects, to identify what changes need to be made. At times, Six Sigma processes may reveal that in addition to needing to improve what we do provide, we may also have to arrive at a deeper understanding of the customer's expectations— and in some cases, back away.

STARTING WITH THE CUSTOMER: DEFINITIONS

A lot of quality control systems jump right into the aspect of improving *quality*—without first defining the customer. Is this such a difficult task? The previous chapter demonstrates that customers can be defined in many ways and that everyone serves a customer in some way. The Accounting Department issues payroll checks for its fellow employee customer; the receptionist serves not only the customer calling in to speak with someone, but also the person receiving calls; the mail room clerk receives and ships packages for its customers throughout the building. All of these people perform functions that, while "support routines" by nature, also fit into the definition of "customer service."

If we attempt to separate different types of service and then treat them differently, what value do we achieve? For example, we may define "customers" as people who give us money in exchange for products or services; and we may view everyone else as supporting that effort. So customer service and the level of quality by which it is executed would be separate and apart from the support service quality we expect from the accountant, receptionist, or mail room clerk. But why? Isn't it possible, in fact practical, to view these employees with the same care and attention we devote to customer service for the cash customer?

Key Point   If customer service and support service are approached with different standards, the whole system fails. It's all customer service, no matter what titles are used.

Six Sigma is designed to operate throughout the entire corporation and, in fact, to alter the entire corporate culture. Customer service, to all intents and purposes, then becomes universal in its nature and application. We may interpret this to mean that anyone providing support services should recognize that their work affects customer service, although indirectly. This is a remote expectation and is not likely to work. After all, if you are *only* an accountant, and you never see a customer, how can you be motivated to improve your customer service attitude? As an alternative, Six Sigma is designed to treat everyone as a frontline customer service employee; that is only practical if and when we recognize that customers are to be found everywhere. Even if they are expressed only in terms of profitability, we cannot distinguish between customer-contact employees and everyone else. The key to bridging this gap is to make customer service a universal concept, and to expect everyone to accept that premise. Putting it another way, "Customer satisfaction is key to long-term profitability and keeping the customer happy is *everybody's* business."[1]

Corporate employees often hear the expression of this idea, but without any real meaning behind it. If we are told, "Everyone has to be concerned with customer service," that is a fine idea; but how do we help the non-marketing employee to improve quality if, at the same time, we tell that employee, "*You* never see a customer"?

Six Sigma enables all corporate employees to play a role in *direct* customer service, because that service mentality should be a part of the very philosophy of how to conduct business. The program—unlike Total Quality Management (TQM)—is based on a few sound principles that encourage corporate-wide customer service attitudes. These include:

✔ *Integration of quality, rather than treatment as a separate routine.* Quality systems of the past were designed as functions on the manufacturing floor, far from management's view or involvement. The programs were isolated, separate not only from management but even from the normal functions of the department. This is a mistake, because in order for any quality program to work, it needs to be integrated, to become part of the way that the department and the company approach all of its work process.

✔ *Requirement that Six Sigma be applied throughout the organization.* Traditional quality programs also were generally viewed as working on the floor where units of production were turned out. Management saw quality control issues as problems for supervisors and foremen and gave them the task of fixing the problem, usually expressed in terms of defect rates. Successful quality control programs were those in which defects were reduced on a particular shift or due to specific quality control changes. Because management was not involved directly within the program, it ultimately fizzled out. Lack of support by management meant that the programs could not be sustained. Any improvements in quality under such a system were only temporary.

✔ *Creation of management support and participation.* It is a vast improvement when management supports a quality control program, as opposed to being apathetic or hostile toward it. In many instances, management viewed such programs as a means for cutting costs only. The all-important bottom line was made the responsibility of the department. With Six Sigma, management is encouraged not only to support the system, but to become an active participant within it. This universal customer service, applied to everyone, changes the way that the task at hand is viewed, whether by a mail room clerk or by a CEO.

✔ *Specific, focused philosophy aimed at achieving specific results.* So many quality control programs expressed ideals but offered no practical means for permanent improvement. The reduction of defects, for example, was the end in itself, and not part of a larger system of doing things. Six Sigma is a quality control program based on a focused philosophy that is meant to change the very outlook of all employees.

✔ *Goals-based strategies in quality-related projects.* Among the failures of traditional quality control programs was the lack of actual goals. "Reducing defects" is not truly a goal in the permanent sense, because it does not address the real problems within a production department. These problems include, among others, boredom coming from repetitive work, low morale or poor attitude, and lack of adequate training. When we move beyond the manufacturing and production model into the service industries, we run into problems if we do not understand how to develop and implement goals. We run into even greater problems when a majority of employees have no end-user customer contact. Developing specific goals related to improving quality helps to focus people and mold them into a customer support point of view.

Key Point In defining solutions to problems, we need to make sure we know not only what we would like to see by way of improved output; we also need to make sure we understand the full range of problems.

We may also be operating with an overly narrow definition of "customer service." We tend to think of defects in terms of failure to meet minimum expectations; but in practice, meeting the customer's requirements or expectations could mean doing *less* in some respects. The definition of a customer's requirements depends on the circumstances. We cannot merely assume that meeting or beating expectations is going to be acceptable.

Example: A bakery supplied pastries and breads to several local stores. One store required delivery by 6 A.M. every Monday, Wednesday, and Saturday. Initially, the bakery recognized only one form of defect worth avoiding: missing the 6 A.M. deadline. As part of its effort to maintain the highest level of customer service, it was able to make on-time deliveries without fail. The system went too far, however, when the bakery began delivering its perishable goods one to two days *early*. Because the store was unable to sell the excess, the goods went stale and could not be sold at all. The customer was dissatisfied with the bakery's level of service. No late delivery, as the sole definition of defect-free service, had to be modified. Excessively *early* delivery was defective as well.

Example: A car dealership followed up on its sale of every vehicle with a telephone call to the customer, to ensure that the experience was positive. The manufacturer also telephoned each customer. Dealer and manufacturer also followed up with a written survey, asking customers to answer a few questions. The system was excellent for the minority of customers who wanted to complain about service; however, with the majority who were satisfied, the excessive contacts were irritating. While less tangible than many other service defects, the unwanted after-sale contact was a form of defect. It would have been adequate to invite comment once and to coordinate between manufacturer and dealer so that both did not necessarily contact the same customers.

In these examples, we realize that the definition of "customer requirement" is not a simple matter. Six Sigma is based on defining specific goals, so it is perfectly suited to addressing the problem, beginning by defining customer expectations. A store does not want early delivery of bakery items, and satisfied customers do not want to be deluged with follow-up inquiries from dealer *and* manufacturer. In whatever way you define your customer, understanding the practical requirements is a good starting point for developing (1) your own customer service program and (2) defining your own customer, even if you never sell your company's goods or services directly.

METHODS OF CUSTOMER RESPONSE

The customer—in both the traditional sense and in the broader sense—is going to react to poor service in predictable ways. They may communicate, walk or complain. The three alternatives, and their components, are summarized in Figure 2.1.

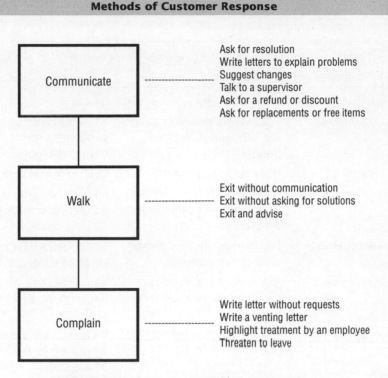

FIGURE 2.1 Customer complaint responses.

To summarize these possible outcomes when expectations are not met, we refer to the chart in Table 2.1, which shows variations for traditional customers and for internal customers (such as fellow employees, for example).

Whether you are dealing with the traditional customer or an internal customer, the responses will fit. With a Six Sigma approach to quality improvements, we want to begin by identifying defects in procedures. By identifying all interactions as being between providers and customers, we can also apply a customer service-style response to all defects. This improves our ability to understand how and why customers respond. It also helps us to treat internal customers with the same care and concern as we treat the traditional customer base.

TABLE 2.1 Customer Reactions to Defects, Two Versions		
Form of Response	Traditional Customer	Internal Customer
Communicate		
Ask for resolution	Ask service provider to fix the problem or replace goods	Ask employee or supervisor for improvements
Write letters	Write to headquarters	Draft internal memos
Suggest changes	Offer ideas for improvement to eliminate problems	Suggestion program or quality assurance plans
Talk to a supervisor	Demand to speak with the employee's supervisor	Talk to supervisor of the employee's department
Ask for refund	Ask for money back or for discount coupon for future use	Request credit on inter-department allocations
Ask for replacement	Ask for another item or one of equal value	Request a different employee or resource to be assigned
Walk		
Exit without communication	Go to competitors for future purchases	Stop asking for assistance due to poor performance
Exit without asking for solutions	Go to competitors and inform company of your decision	Advise of defect or do not ask for solutions
Exit and advise	Go to competitor and explain only if asked	Stop using internal service and explain only if asked
Complain		
Write letters without requests	Explain problem to management without asking for response	Draft internal memo with no suggestions for change
Write a venting letter	Use communication to express anger or frustration	Write memo to complain without suggestions for change
Highlight treatment by an employee	Name offending employee in the letter, ask for management action	Write memo to complain about specific employee problems
Threaten to leave	Write letter threatening to give future business to competitor	Write memo threatening to use other resources, or to resign

Key Point It is easy to assume that customers always respond in the same way to poor service. A more dangerous assumption is that customers must be happy . . . because no one is hearing from them.

For example, most people already know that the *worst* scenario is to fail to respond to a customer complaint—whether outside the organization or within it. For example, a company selling retail office supplies delivered the wrong goods to a customer. The corporate headquarters promised to fix the problem but never did. In this situation, you are better off not making a promise at all. An irritated customer in such a situation started out communicating the problem, but ended up walking. So the customer service response ensured that the customer would be lost permanently. This presents us with at least two separate defects. First, the original problem occurred and is worth investigating. We would want to find out why the wrong goods were shipped out; identify the root causes; and figure out the cost of such mistakes. These investigative steps are part of a thorough Six Sigma project aimed at reducing the defect as much as possible to avoid future problems of that nature. Second—and perhaps a more serious problem—was the failure to follow through with a promise to the customer. This problem may be more difficult to identify because the actual failure was human error. How do you reduce future instances of human error within a customer service department? The solution, of course, is to figure out methods for documenting customer contacts and ensuring a satisfactory (and fast) response, *including* coming through with any promises made. The cost associated with this second defect is easy to identify: The customer is lost forever and, in fact, is out there in the world telling everyone about the bad experience—a walking negative ad for the company.

The same arguments apply within the organization. Our customer service should excel in order to reduce costs and personal frustration, and to make everyone's job smoother. Of course, we cannot always walk when we are dissatisfied as internal customers. For example, if the accounting department promises to reimburse your travel expenses within a week and you have not gotten your check three weeks later, how do you walk? Short of resigning, you really have no alternative but to try to resolve the problem directly with the people in the Accounting Department. If those employees have no clue about the extent of problems they are creating, and if they do *not* adopt a customer service attitude, then you are going to have a problem getting a positive response. However, the key advantage of an effective Six Sigma program is that it does instill a company-wide improved attitude. Not everyone would call this customer service; but by whatever name it is given, if the program does improve attitude and internal response, then it is a positive change that benefits everyone.

For example, the Accounting Department might approach the problem from a purely cost-based point of view. The question in evaluating the problem could be: What does it cost the Accounting Department when reimbursement checks are not sent on a timely basis? A study of the time employees spend on the telephone or answering memos is costly, and prevents those employees from doing other jobs. If the conclusion of the study reveals that collectively, an accounting department is spending 37 hours per week dealing with employees, vendors, and other divisions on matters of late payment or nonpayment of bills, then the costs are easily identified. That is the equivalent of one employee's full-time salary. While this is an example only, it makes the point: Every defect has associated costs, and those costs often are far greater than we might assume at first glance. The costs can be even more specific.

Example: The Accounts Payable Department in a corporation, which owned several retail stores as well as wholesale operations, was in the practice of sending out checks to vendors at the far end of the payment cycle. The employee responsible for timing of payments spent a lot of time on the telephone with vendors making their second or third request for payment. This problem, recognized to be costly in terms of employee labor time, was addressed by the employee who dealt with the vendors directly. The solution: to make all payments within 10 days if vendors offered a discount. Most of the vendors were providing terms of "2 percent–10, net 30" and considering the dollar volume of those payments, the savings were considerable. The corporation had the working capital to make the improvement, so the idea was practical. The remainder of payments were made within the 30-day cycle. Within two months, the level of follow-up calls about late payments had fallen to almost zero.

While this particular example was not the topic of a Six Sigma project, it does demonstrate the type of thinking that goes into the solution-oriented approach. Rather than spending a lot of time dealing with an ongoing problem, the employee realized that the solution was far simpler. It saved money in two ways. It made his time more productive, and it took advantage of discount offers for timely payment.

Customers think in a particular way and expect providers to sign on to that thinking. An example of this is found in the practice of offering discounts for timely payment. A vendor offers a 2 percent discount if you will pay your bill within 10 days. The vendor expects the Accounts Payable Department to take advantage of the incentive, knowing that 2 percent adds up to a large dollar volume among many vendors. So when a company sends out payments 45 or even 60 days late, it is frustrating— not only because of the cash flow problems caused by late payment, but also because the company has not responded to the timely payment incentive.

Key Point If you want to improve quality, you have to first understand what the customer thinks is important, and what the customer thinks of you. Do you measure up to the customer's standards?

One concept often used in Six Sigma is that of including customer data in the process of changing systems, developing or modifying procedures internally, and overall response. This is usually applied solely to traditional customers, but the effects can be impressive when also applied internally. Once the accountant, receptionist, and mail room clerk accept the premise that other employees are *their* customers, a very noticeable change occurs. Those employees look at their routines in a different light.

For internal employees—at least as much as for traditional ones—the big question comes down to whether both sides have matching priorities. For example, if you have submitted an expense report and the Accounting Department promised payment "within a week," your expectation is that you will have a check within a week. However, the Accounting Department's priorities may be different. For example, the individual may have felt compelled to tell you "within a week" because experience has shown that if it takes longer, people complain. However, the normal accounting cycle is to process payments on a semimonthly batch cycle and a batch may have been processed within the past few days—meaning the payment request that comes in today will not be issued for another two weeks (followed by the need for review, signature, and ultimately sending out, a total of up to three weeks from the day the request comes in). Anything outside the normal accounting payment cycle is an exception, and exceptions take time throughout the payment system. In fact, the supervisor in that department may have laid down a requirement that all internal payments are to be made within the batch cycles without exception. This is an ill-advised policy, but typical of the kinds of internal decisions that are made all the time, to great detriment all around.

In this case, the expectations and requirements of each side in the transaction do not match. So we have identified the need to fix the problem. Under the Six Sigma approach, all quality projects are addressed in a five-part system called DMAIC (design, measure, analyze, improve, control), which is explored in detail in Chapter 4. In the preceding example, we have a relatively clear-cut problem of a disconnect in priorities between an employee expecting timely reimbursement, and an accounting department operating in an inflexible batch payment system. Both sides have a point of view; they both live with priorities; and the problem can be fixed with minimal trouble and cost. In fact, because the defect is actually creating more cost and not saving money, the Six Sigma solution would also demonstrate a cost savings as a benefit of change.

The Accounting Department set up its batch system in the belief that cutting individual checks would create more work. Everyone in the company would expect their checks to be issued while they waited, causing unending delays and creating a system in which exceptions would become the rule. There is a compromise, and it is remarkably simple. However, we often need the formality of an objective Six Sigma evaluation—DMAIC—to recognize the rather obvious solutions.

In this example, familiar to many, the problem comes down to an inflexible procedure in the Accounting Department. It appears as an unwillingness to deal with exceptions to payment batch cycles based on the desire to avoid extra cost. The irony, of course, is that as a consequence, department employees are constantly dealing with frustrated, angry people who do not understand the difficulty in processing a check request with the required approval, review, actual cutting of the check, signature, and recording. From the Accounting Department's point of view, inflexibility is required in the name of efficiency. But from the individual who was promised a check within one week, the system is anything but efficient.

The solution to this problem involves a series of changes, including:

✔ Employees in the Accounting Department should not make promises they cannot keep. Because the person expecting payment is a *customer*, the worst thing Accounting can do is promise something that cannot be delivered.

✔ The batch system should be modified to a weekly basis. The two existing batches (let us call these "major" batches) are designed for processing the normal volume of payments to vendors. The two new interim batches (or "minor" batches) are not checks needed sooner than the two- to three-week cycle required to process a payment from beginning to end. With this simple change, the actual delivery of a payment can be promised more realistically. With weekly batches, payment should never take more than two weeks.

✔ The nature of the payment cycle should be explained to all employees. It is not a simple matter of cutting a check while they wait, because such exceptions would add costs to the accounting process; and exceptions would add considerably to the cost of processing payments. Once employees understand what is involved in processing—and the need for batch processing—they are more likely to accept a maximum of a two-week waiting period.

✔ An informal payment system for relatively small payments can be initiated. This can be set up as a petty cash fund to be used for reimbursements under $100, for example, so that employees are not expected to wait two weeks for small payments; and the Accounting Department does not have to incur the costs. Processing a $30 check costs the same as processing a $3,000 check, so an alternative method for handling small payments saves time and money.

The value in thinking of internal employee interactions as provider–customer interactions is twofold. First, it improves communication internally. Second, it helps us to better develop a system for working with traditional customers. By understanding expectations and requirements on both sides of a transaction, we all do a better job. If we do not understand the problem, then we are going to have difficulty arriving at a solution.

Key Point Are administrative employees in the "customer service" business? They had better be, or you will not be able to define expectations and requirements.

Example: Customers complained that in spite of sales reps promising delivery of products within three days from receipt of orders, actual shipments were not arriving for up to two weeks. The initial response by the Vice President of Marketing was, "What's wrong with those guys down in Shipping?" It would seem apparent that the Shipping and Receiving Department was dropping the ball. Why is it so difficult to get orders out on time?

On further analysis, it came to light that the problem was far more complex. It included several elements:

✔ Sales reps were not delivering paperwork on time, often not even within the promised three-day shipping deadline.

✔ Inefficiency in the Marketing Department often caused additional processing delays, so that a one- to two-day lapse was occurring before Shipping and Receiving got the order.

✔ Further inefficiency in inventory procedures caused excessive backordering of goods, so that the three-day promises could not be kept because those goods were not on hand.

✔ Shipping problems included late receipt of basic shipping supplies. Because ordering was not done until the department ran out of packaging supplies, delays occurred at least twice per month while the department was waiting for their own deliveries from the vendor.

✔ Deliveries of shipping supplies often were held up for additional days because the vendor had not yet been paid for last month's deliveries—and refused to ship until payment was received.

The extent of this problem is illustrated in Figure 2.2.

In a traditional approach to quality control problems, it is not difficult to figure out how this problem would have been handled. The Vice President of Marketing would have called the manager of Shipping and Receiving and said, "You have to fix this problem. I want those orders to go out within three days, no exceptions."

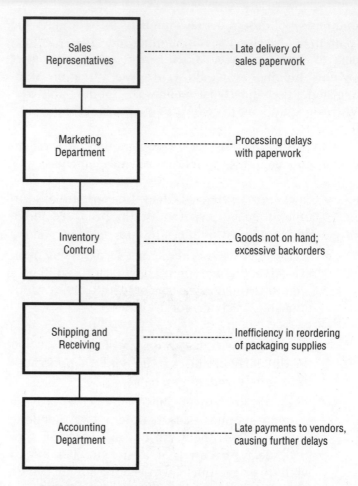

FIGURE 2.2 Multidepartmental quality problem.

Assuming that the problem was being caused by one department means that blame is never shared, the extent of the problem is not analyzed, and ultimately, the problem cannot be fixed because it is not fully understood. It is rare for a defect to be caused in a single department or by one employee only. As the previous example shows, many seemingly simple and obvious problems have a number of components. The fix of such problems requires a thorough study and development of the extent of the problem. The solution has to involve fixing the problem at all of its stages. The delays are not caused by defects in any one place; if we are to assign blame, there is enough to go around. The Six Sigma structure (see Chapter 4) for identifying and fixing problems is effective because it begins with no assumptions; it is designed to study the problem and trace it through from beginning to end. As a result, the solution makes sense because it fixes *all* the defects, not just the ones that are most visible.

In the example, the problems extended over several departments and involved sales reps, marketing, shipping and receiving, inventory control, and accounting. The entire cycle contributed to the problem. In spite of the tendency to see defects as being relatively simple to fix, this demonstrates the opposite: The promise to ship goods within three days of the sale was not a difficult idea on the surface of it; but as we have discovered, the entire system fell apart and the chain of defects was more than just a problem in one department. In fact, we discovered upon analysis that the problems were far more complex and far-reaching than they appeared at first. The analysis of this specific case and the solution are provided as a detailed example in Chapter 6.

QUANTIFYING THE IDEAL

In the best of all possible worlds, we would be able to eliminate defects once and for all, deal with other employees, customers, and vendors in harmony, and execute transactions without any trouble whatsoever. But we also have to remember the warning "The optimist proclaims that we live in the best of all possible worlds; and the pessimist fears this is true."[2]

Whether we confront problems believing in the optimistic view that we can fix them, or resigning ourselves to the pessimistic view that problems themselves are going to be endless, we must return to a basic assumption: that among our roles and duties, problem solving belongs near the top of the list. Because problems take up our time, cost money, and negatively affect our morale, we need to strive for solution. Eliminating or reducing defects also reduces our time commitment, saves money, and improves our morale. So in addition to the obvious benefits inherent in a successful quality program, we also expect to see personal benefits and rewards.

Key Point Problem solving should be at the top of everyone's priority list. In solving problems, we all deal with quality issues daily.

In one classic best-selling book, the advice is put forth that problems can be solved in one minute. This theory is based on the idea that a "one-minute goal" is focused and clarified and, like its related topics of one-minute praise and one-minute reprimand, the purpose is to demand that everyone get to the bottom line, quickly.[3]

In some respects, one-minute managing can be quite effective. However, in other respects, it is the antithesis of Six Sigma. We already know that defects cannot be resolved with a quick and dirty one-minute review; in the real world, we need to be more analytical and methodical, to ensure that we thoroughly understand the elements of a problem before we rush to a solution. In the practical application of one-minute managing, the effect is to cut managers out of the loop. Employees who have problems (in other words, the manager's "customers") will stop seeking help from the manager if they are limited to a one-minute session to express the problem. There are appropriate applications for one-minute managing; quality control is not one of them.

Imagine the discussion about the problem of the three-day delivery promise. How could an employee and manager resolve such a problem in a one-minute discussion, or in increments of a one-minute review? The conversation might go something like this:

Sales Rep: I have to talk to you about a serious problem.
VP, Marketing: (*turning over an egg timer*) You have one minute. Begin.
Sales Rep: I've been promising that orders are going to be shipping within three days from placement, you

know, the idea we talked about at last month's one-minute sales meeting.

VP, Marketing: Sure I remember. How's that going?

Sales Rep: Orders aren't being shipped on time. In fact, they're taking up to two weeks, more in some cases.

VP, Marketing: What's wrong with those guys down in Shipping?

Sales Rep: I don't know, but my customers are pretty upset. If we don't get this problem fixed, I'm going to start losing business.

VP, Marketing: (*dialing the phone*) I'll take care of this right now. (*pause*) Hi, Stan. This is Ed. I understand you're not getting those orders shipped within three days. You better get that problem fixed, pronto. We're losing business up here. (*pause*) No, I don't want to hear about delays and inventory problems and don't try to blame this on Accounting. How hard is it to send out an order? That's your job; let's get it done. (*hangs up phone*)

Sales Rep: I hope that helps. I don't see why it should be so hard.

VP, Marketing: Well, you know, they don't deal with customers directly, so they just don't get it. We have to lean on them now and then to make sure they do their job.

That's one minute. Not knowing the full extent of the problem, it seems like a harsh, but direct solution-oriented management approach. It is obvious to both the sales rep and to the Vice President of Marketing that the Shipping and Receiving Department is the problem. As a one-minute manager, an expedient solution is both desirable and effective. However, we also know from an analysis of the many contributing causes to this problem that no one-minute meeting or assertive telephone call is going to solve this problem. It is naïve to accept the premise that all problems can be dealt with simplistically; however, that is a popular and common belief. It explains and demonstrates why so many half-baked quality control programs do not work.

Key Point   If you think you can solve problems quickly, simply, and in a vacuum, then you have not yet defined the problem. Another look is worthwhile.

In this example, the marketing and sales folks were operating on the premise that the Shipping and Receiving Department did not understand customer service, because they never saw a customer. Under a Six Sigma approach to quality control, this problem would have been dealt with on an entirely different premise. Forgetting for the moment the theoretical appeal of one-minute management, the solution would require definition of the problem. The VP, Marketing would have started out by contacting the manager of Shipping and Receiving and saying, "I understand we're having problems getting orders shipped within three days. I think you and I should meet with the head of Sales and find out why we're having this problem."

This approach does not assume that the problem resides solely in Shipping and Receiving. It is focused on the problem and not on any individuals; it also leaves open the possibility that the problem extends beyond the Shipping and Receiving Department. In this variation, the VP, Marketing recognizes that such problems are rarely so isolated, and also that a one-minute strategy is not going to resolve the difficulty or end the problem.

We might prefer the ideal world, in which problems are easily identified and solved, and everyone interacts in complete harmony. In our real corporate world, that is rarely the case and, perhaps, such an ideal would be far less interesting as well. Under a Six Sigma approach, we suggest a different version of the "ideal world." Under this version, we are aware of the *ideal*—a defect-free environment. We also accept the reality that it is impossible to achieve a defect-free operating environment. Processes do not work perfectly, but if we are aware of the ideal, we can certainly raise the defect-free outcomes by improving processes. In the example of the problems of three-day shipping defects, we have to cure a number of defects that will be found in every department involved in the transaction. We can assume that few transactions are going through defect-free because the problems are so wide-spread. In fact, it is unrealistic under the present operating environment for the sales rep to promise three-day delivery; it simply is not going to happen. So the many problems have to be fixed within a single effort; it makes no sense to put the entire problem on Shipping and Receiving because that is not the only place where the system has fallen apart. The ideal belief that a single phone call can fix the problem does not work in the real world, where virtually all problems cross departmental lines, with a cause and effect complicating the remote quality effort. Only a company-wide Six Sigma approach will permanently fix problems, because defects tend to have many tentacles and to exist in many departments.

THE NATURE OF SERVICE

The concept of "customer service"—and for the purposes of understanding Six Sigma, this means that everyone has a customer—has been around for a long time. A cynical point of view about customer service is that it is a method aimed at (1) keeping customers happy, (2) improving profits, and (3) minimizing the hassle of complaints. A person with a more enlightened point of view recognizes that in fact, *service* is an approach to work, an attitude we bring with us each morning, and a philosophical and cultural point of view. It should achieve the three benefits that the cynical observer believes are at the core of a service program; and it should also achieve much more as well.

Key Point Service—at all levels—is a point of view, a philosophical approach that is more than responding to complaints, improving profits, and reducing workload. Service is, or should be, at the core of every organization. If your company does not recognize this, your competitors will.

The ability to view an issue in the same way a customer views it is essential in order to create a high-quality environment. So a sales representative succeeds if he or she is able to comprehend what motivates a customer. For some, it is a desire to buy a quality product; for others, the motivation is based on envy, fear, jealousy, or material greed; and for still others, it is a desire for acknowledgment from someone else. So a person buys a status automobile as a way of telling his neighbors that he is affluent; and a family pays twice as much for a house in a different neighborhood for the same reasons. In some cases, a customer responds to the salesperson rather than wanting to make an impression on someone else. So when closing the sale, the rep may say, "You are going to be very happy with this decision" or something along those lines. Assurance may be what that customer wants. So the observant sales rep is able to judge the customer.

Your internal customer also has the need for some form of acknowledgment or satisfaction. Some want their power and control to be recognized; others respond to flattery or merely to being asked for something with respect and courtesy. Anyone who has to work with other people knows that figuring out what makes them tick is the key to getting what you need and want.

Example: The Accounting Department is notoriously slow in delivering reimbursement checks to sales reps. The reaction among many is to speak to the accounting supervisor abusively. "If I treated my customers this way, I'd be out of business" or "You accountants would never survive out there in the real world" are common statements, made in anger. However, one rep sees that the problem is lack of respect. He always seems to get his check on time because he has made an effort. He has invited the accounting supervisor to lunch, stopped to chat with the supervisor, and always asked for speedy payment with courtesy. He also gets his checks in half the time that most others get theirs, and it is never misrouted in error.

Everyone understands the dynamic in internal relations. It is the *nature of service* that we all react and respond in a predictable manner. This is obvious to the sales and marketing staff, even though they do not apply the same approach to the internal customer in every instance; and the internal customers and providers often are not aware of the nature of service as it affects their performance or their results.

A lot of time and effort is spent in evaluating levels of service and attempting to place the attribute of good service on a chart. This may be useful in some applications. However, with or without the engineering of quality monitoring, the issue is the same: Service includes not only identifying customer requirements; it also has to extend to providing excellence in product or service. We have to ensure that *our* priorities and the customer's priorities match. We will run into instances where they do not match, and in those instances there has to be some form of adjustment in the requirements, on one side or both. For example, the sales rep wants an expense reimbursement check within one week or less, and the Accounting Department has to conform to periodic batch processing restrictions. This disconnect—and many others like it—are perfect challenges for Six Sigma, because a company-wide approach considers all departmental requirements and participation, and identifies the various contributors to the problem. So a solution is likely to be derived in both functional and design elements.

In Six Sigma, the *Quality Function Deployment (QFD)* refers to the conversion from a customer's requirements, to specific *design requirements* within the internal process. For example, a customer may require a level of service or a specific product attribute that the company does not currently provide. The design elements and features in manufacture, handling, processing, packaging, pricing, and delivery of the product might need to be altered to meet these expectations.

Example: The manufacturer of electronic equipment included a 10-year warranty with all of its sales. One customer—in fact, the company's largest customer—wanted a lifetime warranty. The problem for the company was expressed in the question "How do we label one series of finished products with a 10-year warranty and the other

Quality Function Deployment (QFD) a conversion of processes required when a customer's requirements are not compatible with current operating procedures; designed to adjust those processes to ensure quality improvements.

design requirements the process elements of products or services, which may need to be adjusted to meet the customer's requirements.

with a lifetime warranty?" The problem included deciding how many to label in each fashion, because the metal label was attached to each unit during the manufacturing process itself. Having to go back later and add labeling would add a lot of cost to the process. A Six Sigma team studied the problem and arrived at a solution. They studied the history of the equipment and concluded that no units had ever been returned under the warranty program. Because the quality was so high, the team recommended that the lifetime warranty should be provided on *all* units. This not only satisfied the requirements of the largest customer, it improved the service level to everyone else as well. The functional requirements of one customer led to a change in the design elements of the product.

Key Point   A solution does not have to be complex. But the process of defining the problem often is, because it may not be well understood until it is analyzed.

This is a typical situation. The solution was simple once it was studied carefully. Initially, the problem was viewed as one of inventory management. After a study of the situation, the team realized that the customer's requirement presented an opportunity that had not been considered before. Their solution eliminated the need for a different inventory tracking system or for added cost in the manufacture process.

CORPORATE GOVERNANCE AS CUSTOMER SERVICE

The big changes in recent years in the field of "corporate governance" have brought up new customer service issues. Governance refers to the ways that corporations communicate with investors, employees, and regulators in compliance with the law, listing standards, and investor needs. Even though corporate governance is recognized as an important attribute in determining quality of service, it is not often defined in terms of customer service.

The Sarbanes–Oxley Act of 2002 changed many of the rules under which corporations and executives were required to provide information to investors and to others. In many respects, the Act defined a customer service approach that corporations would be required to adopt (in addition to attempting to prevent a repeat of many abuses among corporate executives, accounting firms, and analysts that came to light in 2001 and 2002). For example, the new law "requires steps to enhance the direct responsibility of senior corporate management for financial reporting and for the quality of financial disclosures made by public companies."[4]

This "direct responsibility" means that the officers of companies are required to *personally* certify the accuracy of financial statements. In a very real sense, this represents a government-enforced form of customer service. If we recognize that the investor is a customer of the company whose stock he or she owns, then what are the customer requirements and expectations? These would include:

✔ A desire for the stock value to rise over time, based on a perceived fundamental value in the company and as reflected in its financial reports. (Translation: If an investor is to make a decision, it should be an *informed* decision, which often means analyzing financial reports to identify long-term value.)

✔ An expectation that the financial reports are, in fact, accurate. (This expectation has not always been met in the past by corporations like Enron, for example.)

✔ A requirement of reliance upon top executives and the board of directors to protect the interests of the investor (customer).

These customer requirements among investors are logical and reasonable. The Act was designed to protect investors in public companies. The government has often adopted a similar role. The Food and Drug Administration

(FDA) approves drugs for public sale; the United States Department of Agriculture (USDA) inspects meat processing plants to ensure that the national food supply is clean and safe; and speed limits are intended to reduce the number of traffic accidents and fatalities.

In these various forms of government involvement, the provider/customer interaction is complicated. The regulatory role played by the government not only requires compliance with specific standards; in many respects, it adds another layer of customer service, complicating the definition of service itself. In Figure 2.3, the interactions of the three players demonstrate this point.

In this illustration we see that the regulators impose standards on the product or service being offered. Virtually all the products or services bought by consumers include some form of regulatory oversight, government licensing, or other types of standards. Even the internal customer has such protection, in the form of laws regarding employment standards and labor relations, discrimination, wrongful discharge, hostile work environments,

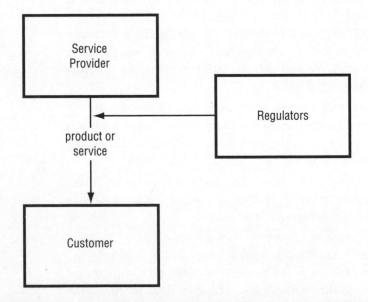

FIGURE 2.3 Customer service and the regulatory environment.

and more. The involvement of a regulator creates many levels of customer and provider, including:

✔ Service provider (originator of product or service) and end-user customer

✔ Service provider and regulator (whose requirements relate to forms of compliance)

✔ Regulator and end user (whose requirements include dependence on quality assurance provider via oversight, licensing, inspections, and enforcement of the law)

Key Point To evaluate *your* role in customer service, begin by defining *your* customer, both external and internal. Who depends on you for service?

If we are to define "service" universally, we have to also accept a broader than usual definition of the customer. We have to assume that anyone who receives a service or a product (or who pays taxes, for that matter, in exchange for certain oversight functions provided by the government) is a customer. This includes end users, other employees and departments, subcontractors, and regulators. All of these interests receive a benefit in the form of a product or a service, and all have to be considered in our definition of "service." This is a starting point for defining the value of Six Sigma, and its purpose. We cannot view "service" as belonging only to an external customer. If we do that, improved quality is impossible. We have to also ensure that the internal processes meet customer requirements on every level; and that to the extent an internal service provider is also a customer, their requirements have to be met as well. This is the only approach that will enable a quality program to succeed.

THINKING LIKE A CUSTOMER

The concept of defining many groups or individuals as customers is fine by itself. But how do we change our point of view and method of operation to understand our customers in their various forms? How do we learn to "think like the customer?"

This is not as difficult a task as it might seem. In fact, everyone who works with other people already knows all about requirements, demands, and expectations. These attributes define all work-related interactions. We cannot merely expect people to function within the corporation in a customer service mode without providing a real framework for that change. Six Sigma may prove the value of service, but only when it is applied within the environment. Some leaders have tried to instill a change in the morale and motivation of employees with words alone, or with the institution of isolated quality control programs; this does not work.

In order for quality control to provide real improvements on all levels, we also need to evaluate all problems on a corporate-wide basis. If management assigns the rank and file the task of "improving quality"— whether expressed in terms of cost savings, fewer defects, faster response time, or other measurable results—the idea is doomed to fail. When the problem is given to the department but management takes no part in solving the problem, any perceived solutions will not last; employees will correctly perceive the notion of quality control as a method used by management to squeeze more profit out of the bottom line and, perhaps, to identify ways to cut expenses (translation: to lay off employees). Such suspicions are well founded in situations where (1) management has taken the same course in the past, (2) management expresses no desire to *lead* the effort or take part in its implementation, and (3) there exists no framework for defining the problem and its whole scope. Consider the example provided earlier in this chapter of the problem with getting orders shipped within three days. If management simply views this as a Shipping and Receiving Department problem, it cannot solve the *real* problem, which includes components of defects in many other departments as well: Sales, Marketing, Accounting and, ultimately, Management. The problem with Management, in this application, is in the failure to lead the quality effort. As long as Management holds onto the traditional view—that problems are to be fixed by the department itself—the more complex defects do, indeed, go all the way to the top. Effective management in this situation requires, as a first step, leading the company into a process that will be able to really fix the problem. This is where Six Sigma becomes so effective. This idea—that management has everything to do with creating a quality control program—is addressed in the next chapter.

Outside-In Thinking

I was thinking about the real meaning of "customer service" one day while I was waiting in line at a very large retail store's return desk. One clerk was on duty and approximately 15 people were waiting; to make matters worse, the clerk was moving as slowly as humanly possible. I found myself imagining that this system was set up by design, to discourage people from coming back for refunds. Then the one thing I was not expecting actually happened. The clerk went on her break and was replaced by another, who was even slower. At this point I realized that, in fact, for that store "customer service" was viewed as a means of forcing customers to suffer through the lengthy return procedure only if they were willing to wait a long, long time. It was worse than going to the Department of Motor Vehicles.

Once we begin to appreciate the true nature of interaction with the customer, the Six Sigma idea takes shape. That customer service approach, which defines quality in *all* our interactions, both internal and external, is the foundation of the quality control idea itself. If we do not have a customer to whom we want to improve service, then what is the purpose of trying to upgrade quality?

A retail store *should* make returns easy, for example. Why can't items be returned at the register, for example? Why can't a special return desk be staffed by more than one person? Why are the return desk employees always the slowest-moving ones? When we have a negative customer experience, we have to analyze the motivation of the person providing that service, before we can address the question "How can we improve it?" The reality could be that from the point of view of the provider, no improvement is necessary.

One of the chronic problems in customer service is an unawareness of the problem itself. If revenues and earnings are on the rise, why go through the self-examination to improve customer service? Obviously, it is working. And if revenues and earnings are falling, it is easy to blame competition, the economy, or interest rates and to avoid needing to take a hard look at problems in customer service. Even though a review of service problems can make everyone's life easier *and* improve the bottom line, we usually find a lot of resistance to that idea, whether working with cash-paying customers or the department down the hall.

A FRESH LOOK AT INTERNAL PROBLEMS

Why is the Six Sigma process set up to begin with a thorough *defining* process? The very approach is based on the belief that in order to fix a problem, we have to first understand it thoroughly. In so many instances, what we believe to be the problem turns out to be nothing more than a symptom of something far bigger. Consider the example of the problem: "The Shipping and Receiving Department is not filling orders within three days, as promised by our sales representatives." At first, this appears to be a problem isolated within one department but upon further investigation, we discover that many departments contribute to a far larger problem. So the solution has to be broader as well.

The real definition of any quality program has to depend on how it is approached. If a vice president demands that a single department fix its problems without realizing the involvement of many other departments, then the whole idea is doomed to fail. This is the *status quo* in so many companies. Executives are continually writing memos and passing them along instructing fixes for *perceived* problems and, in response, some actions are taken. What is lacking in that whole process is a true understanding of the problem. The entire approach is inefficient.

Key Point Understanding the full scope of the problem is a starting point; if we do not go through that step, we cannot solve the problem because we do not understand it yet.

If we are interested in efficiency—in the name of quality or just to simplify our own lives—then we can define Six Sigma as a method for simplifying efficiency. That may take some work and the more time we spend in defining and examining the problem before we begin solving it, the better that process is going to work. If our goal is to put efficiency into processes, then we can begin to develop working models for *effective* outcomes. These terms—"efficiency" and "effectiveness" and other terms like them—are used a lot internally, but without our really defining what they mean. What is an efficient process and what is an effective outcome?

To proceed into an examination of how Six Sigma can help us to improve our customer service levels, we will begin with definitions of these terms. An "efficient process" is one that achieves the end result with minimum time and effort, and for minimum cost. For example, a retail store may use a returns desk, which means a bottleneck of customers creates ill will. It takes too long and does not work well. The returns desk is not staffed adequately for the customer demand and, once they get to the front of the line, the paperwork is excessive. This is an inefficient process and the store needs to review its procedures with the customer in mind. In an "efficient" process, we are able to reduce paperwork and the time a customer has to wait for what it needs from you (a refund, a piece of paper, a return phone call, a report, or a product, for example). The easier this process moves along, the more efficient it will be viewed by the customer.

An "effective outcome" is one that meets the customer's requirements. What if you have to wait for half an hour only to discover you have been in the wrong line the whole time? Obviously, you are not going to be happy with the outcome. What if you are in the right line but, because of something beyond your control, the person you are waiting to see is not able to give you what you want? Again, there is no effective outcome. By the time you do finalize the transaction, you will be so frustrated by the inefficiency of the process that the end result "customer service" is lost in that process itself.

We cannot have an effective outcome without an efficient process. This is the whole point of examining current processes with customers in mind. We need to identify not only the procedural aspects of the process; we also need to examine how the customer feels about the entire matter.

Example: You discover an error on your credit card bill. You telephone the toll-free customer service number and you are left on Hold by three different people. After 45 minutes, you finally get someone who is able to tell you that you need to submit a written summary.

In this case, the transaction might be defined by the company as functionally successful. The customer got an answer to the telephone inquiry, so by that definition it was a successful customer service process. As the customer, however, your frustration level was caused by several aspects of the transaction and the inefficiencies of the process:

✔ You spent 45 minutes on Hold.
✔ People you spoke to did not know the answers to your questions.
✔ When the transaction ended, you still needed to take another step; the problem was *not* resolved.

The process was inefficient and, from your point of view, the outcome was not effective. So the whole transaction *failed* from a practical point of view. Let us further assume that this company tracks its telephone calls to the customer service center. Your telephone call might be analyzed with a rather singular question: Did the customer get an answer to the question?

If the company assumes that your question was, "How do I get an error removed from my statement?" then the phone call might be defined as successful. But perhaps a better question would be: Did the customer service employee *know the answer* to the customer's question? Another self-critical question could be: How long did the customer remain on the phone before the question was answered? A third could be: Was the issue resolved, or did the customer need to take further action? These questions would point out the inefficiency of the process.

Too many internal analysis of customer service are focused narrowly on outcomes. It does not matter whether an outcome is defined in positive ways if, in fact, the process was inefficient or the outcome only directed the customer to another path, like writing a letter instead of getting the problem resolved by telephone. So many so-called customer service processes involve employees who have not been trained adequately, who do not treat customers with courtesy, or who have no idea about customer service. Many companies understaff their customer service departments so that callers spend most of the call on Hold or speak to someone who does not know how to address their needs. In these situations, the company is probably unaware of the negative impression that customers form of their company, because they are not studying or analyzing the situation. They cannot fix the problem, because they do not know that a problem exists.

Key Point Not understanding a problem is bad enough, but it is far worse when employees do not even know the problem exists—because they have not looked at their own interactions critically.

How do we make effectiveness of outcomes the working model for the job that we do? This idea is at the core of a quality program and Six Sigma—by starting from a point of definition—is designed to achieve the working model result. The steps involved are:

1. Define the problem from the customer's point of view.
2. Identify inefficiencies and their causes.
3. Eliminate the inefficiency to change the outcome.
4. Study the revised outcome.

Example: A mortgage company sent a customer a revised escrow statement. The company made a mistake in calculating the twice-yearly amount payable for property taxes. Instead of listing one-half of the full year's tax liability, it showed the full year's tax as being due twice per year. The revised statement included a bill of $800 for the calculated escrow shortage, due within one month and increased monthly payments $300 higher than before. The borrower telephoned the mortgage company several times and never was able to speak to the same person twice. It took more than three weeks before the problem was fixed.

In this situation, several process inefficiencies contributed to the problem, including:

✔ Lack of review by an individual of the revised escrow statement before it was mailed (the problem of dependence on automated processing, so that errors do not get caught).

✔ Customer service employees who did not know how to fix the problem (the caller was told variously that he had the wrong department, that the change could not be made because the escrow bills were already batched, and that there was no error).

✔ Employees—including a supervisor—were rude to the caller and unresponsive to his requirements (it took three weeks before anyone was able to comprehend the point that it was the mortgage company's error; several employees told the borrower, "This information is entered from the bill sent to us by your local tax collector," which is a way of saying "We didn't make a mistake").

The problem in this case has many aspects, including poorly trained employees, lack of understanding of the problem, lack of empathy for the customer, and an overly complex system in which *their* errors could not be easily fixed. The mortgage company—like so many other service providers—appeared to be dominated by employees with a poor customer service attitude. In other words, it is unlikely that management even knew there was a problem.

If this dilemma were to be studied as a Six Sigma project, the very first step would be to appoint the people to the team who would be able to define the scope of the problem. Perhaps the best way to achieve this would be for someone within the company to simply telephone the Customer Service Department with a question and experience the problem first-hand. This is one way to identify the problem from the customer's point of view: Pose as a customer and experience what actually happens when you telephone the customer service line.

A second step would be to measure what the problem costs the company. This is important because a quality control project can be best defined in terms of how changes eliminate wasted time, resources, and money. So the completion of a reformed process can be pointed to as adding a specific amount to the bottom line. It is interesting that this specific, identifiable change is limited only to the *tangible* benefits. In other words, what difference does it make in terms of profits? If the mortgage company fixed its customer service problems so that it could be more responsive to its customers, it would cut costs. The Six Sigma team could demonstrate that it had saved an exact number of dollars per year. It does not also measure the intangible benefits of improved customer relations, which can be many multiples of benefit to the company. It is those intangibles—the way that customers view a company's customer service—that ultimately defines how well a company is able to compete in the market. This intangible—we can give it the name Disgust Index—is difficult to quantify because companies often do not hear from their customers; those people simply stop doing business and shop for their products or services with the competition.

Even when the initial transaction is inefficient, if the process is set up to catch the problem, the transaction can be saved and converted into an efficient transaction. If this happens before the customer becomes frustrated, then the process works. The most common and chronic problems, however, occur in cases where the company is not at all aware that inefficient customer transactions are causing ineffective outcomes. The possible chain of events is summarized in Figure 3.1.

Note that in this illustration, even the initially inefficient process can be corrected in the *response* phase. Employees have often experienced the situation in which response is passive, unconcerned, and seemingly unaware (or uncaring) about the customer. In those situations, there is no hope of fixing the problem—unless that problem can be discovered and fixed. This assumes, of course,

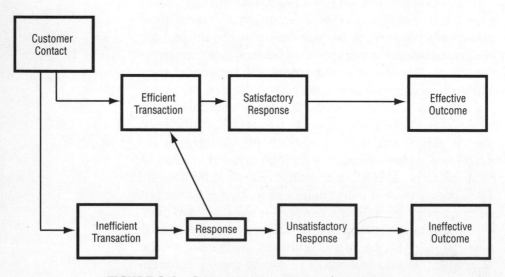

FIGURE 3.1 Customer processes and outcomes.

that the company is, in fact, interested in improving the quality of its customer service.

Key Point   A passive attitude toward customer service will ensure one outcome: loss of that customer.

One internal attitude that often gets in the way of improving customer service is the idea that customer service is not important. The problem of unawareness is bad enough; it is even worse when the employees in the company do not consider the problem worth fixing. For example, the customer service employee in a mortgage company might believe the consumer has no choice but to deal with them because (1) the customers need to borrow the money to buy their homes, (2) everyone gets poor service, so why change? (3) it is too expensive for people to refinance, so those customers are not going anywhere else, even if they wanted to, and (4) even if customers do leave in disgust, business is on the rise; more customers are coming through all the time; and the whole organization is strained and understaffed. In other words, who cares?

Every organization—even those that are today's leaders within an industry—eventually peak out and then decline. As aggressive competitors begin taking away market share, this trend cannot be changed. The common attribute among companies that have grown too large too quickly is the decline of customer service. Once that happens, it is all too easy for a leaner, better-organized competitor to take away momentum.

ORGANIZING THE INTERNAL QUALITY PROGRAM

Most quality programs are aimed at improving service on the way up, as revenues and earnings climb. This is where quality begins to suffer. As volume grows, profits tend to shrink and eventually the whole operation begins to decline. But a quality program can also be designed so that the internal quality program works to prevent that decline.

The reason that companies lose their competitive edge has everything to do with levels of service. Growth—often at the expense of service itself—is not going to sustain the corporate structure because, sooner or later, the decline in service works its way through to the bottom line. Losses replace profits and a reputation for excellence in service is replaced with one for consistently low levels of service. "I guess they got too big" is a common observation about corporations and that observation is right on the money. However, your company can grow without losing its level of service. Using an internal Six Sigma program to identify and define modes of growth (within an excellent service model) is the way to ensure that expansion does not mean the end of profitability (and along with it, the end of positive service reputation).

There is a specific connection between managing internal growth and maintaining excellent customer service. It is not necessary to sacrifice service for growth, in spite of that pattern's being experienced time and again. An internal program based on the Six Sigma strategy, action plan, and service approach (to the entire culture and not only within quality-related projects) enables a company to expand operations in every respect—personnel, product and service lines, geographic influence, facilities, capital—without losing quality in its customer service program.

The three components of the internal program are summarized in Figure 3.2.

Business Process Management, or BPM (see Chapter 1) is the corporate executive-level strategy for the corporate quality program. This is where the decision is made to pursue a permanent change in the corporate culture by applying Six Sigma as a methodology. In comparison, other quality programs are viewed as functional aspects of operations, a way to cut costs by reducing defects, improving efficiency, and making management's job easier, but *without management's involvement* within the program. Under the Six Sigma approach to quality, management begins its BPM strategic approach by also committing to the

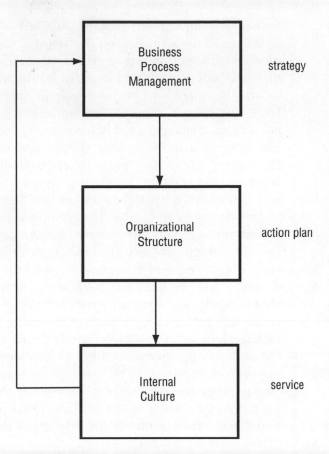

Business
Process
Management   strategy

Organizational
Structure   action plan

Internal
Culture   service

FIGURE 3.2 Components of the internal program.

program in a participatory manner and not just by impos-
ing the program upon the rank and file.

Key Point Management can simply delegate quality to
departments or, as an alternative, management can create
an effective, working system. The second approach has
one advantage over the first: It works.

The second component is the action plan itself,
which is a revision to the organizational structure. We are
used to thinking vertically, with management at the top
and the worker at the bottom. Under Six Sigma, we maintain a chain of command and organizational structure, but

we begin to think in terms of the team rather than the individual, the department, and the division. Under the traditional mode of thinking, each unit (person, department, division) tends to think in terms of self-interest. There is no real incentive for company-wide perspective. At this level, that culture is revised organizationally by the creation of an analytical approach to quality. At this phase, management determines who should take responsibility for training, identifying project areas needing immediate attention, and creating the actual program.

The third component is the revised internal culture and its emphasis on service. Here, employees at all levels within the company are trained to take on a changed view of how things work. The internal culture, often described as a series of departments and individuals who do *not* work cooperatively with one another, can and should work as a company-wide team; and the way to create that is through the Six Sigma service orientation. Management cannot simply mandate that departments are to work together; they have to be changed using a methodical approach. The *scientific method* applies in quality programs as elsewhere. By viewing the change in the corporate culture as the first Six Sigma project to be undertaken, the starting point is to apply the standards of the scientific method.

Why the scientific method? In corporate culture, so many motives, assumptions, and conflicts are in play in any situation, especially one where a major change is being proposed. "How is this going to affect me?" is the unspoken question on everyone's mind. When the CEO announces that the company is going to take on a new company-wide quality control program, few people are going to be happy about the announcement. Even though Six Sigma is vastly different from any other quality program the company has tried before, people are cynical and they will initially view the program suspiciously.

The scientific method works perfectly for the internal program components previously identified: strategy, action plan, and service. No two people are going to share the same perceptions about corporate culture, where they fit within that culture, and to what extent major changes

scientific method
a set of procedures used to objectively evaluate information, to arrive at an accurate conclusion based on initial assumptions, definitions, and tests.

will affect them. As a consequence, all forms of change meet with resistance, often with concerted, fierce, and determined resistance. Six Sigma is a truly revolutionary change. It removes self-interest from the culture, not entirely of course, but enough so that people discover that working from a team approach is rewarding. By taking the first step, management begins to mold a new, fresh point of view. As one writer expressed this idea, "We used to think that revolutions are the cause of change. Actually it is the other way around: change prepares the ground for revolution."[1]

Under the scientific method, change itself is given structure and certainty. This method has four parts: First is observation and definition of the problem. Second is the development of a hypothesis or theory regarding the required solution. Third is the calculation of outcomes you would expect from change, such as increased profits, faster process time, or fewer steps. And fourth is the testing phase, in which the new process or conclusion is tested.

Example: The Accounting Department takes up to three weeks to prepare and deliver reimbursement checks; sales reps would like to get their money within one week. Applying the scientific method and its four steps, the process is:

1. Observe and define: What is the problem and why does it exist?

2. Hypothesis: How can the problem be solved? What processes should be changed?

3. Expectations: What changes in the process would you expect as a result of the changes proposed?

4. Testing: Does the revised procedure solve the problem?

The four steps, summarized in Figure 3.3, show how the scientific method is applied to a Six Sigma project.

The phases are revised one by one. If the hypothesis does not hold up to examination, we return to the first

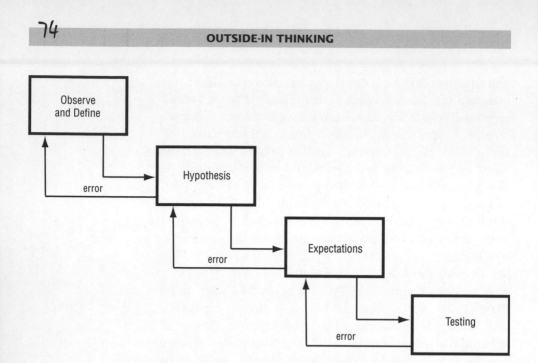

FIGURE 3.3 The scientific method and Six Sigma.

step and redefine. For example, we may believe initially that the problem of slow delivery of checks is caused by inefficiency in the Accounting Department; when the hypothesis is developed, we discover that the department operates by necessity on a batching system, so the problem needs to be reviewed with improved information.

Expectations are similarly reviewed and, if they are found in error, we return to the original hypothesis. For example, we might conclude that the accounting batch cycles need to be made more efficient so that turnaround time is improved. However, when reviewing expectations, we may determine that instead, we need to add additional minor batches in the off-weeks between the two major monthly batches. Finally, when the project changes are tested, we may discover additional errors, requiring a return to outcome expectations.

When all four steps are completed successfully, we will have arrived at a solution that (1) was properly defined, (2) was based on a correct hypothesis, (3) was developed with realistic expectations, and (4) met those expectations in the testing phase.

Key Point Many organizations are focused on *solutions*. It would be far more effective and satisfying if, instead, they were taught to focus on *effective solutions*.

Because Six Sigma is designed on the assumption that we all have customers to serve, this four-step system is nothing less than a methodical way to define customer service, identify problems, and make corrections. For example, if a company whose customers make phone calls *assumes* that "getting the answer to a question" is a satisfactory outcome in a contact transaction, then it does not matter if the customer ends up angry and frustrated. It also does not matter if it takes a long time and numerous phone calls to get that answer. Under the scientific method, the problem would be defined and a hypothesis formed. But the hypothesis would be challenged and found to be flawed if, in fact, the Six Sigma team determined that the problem had more components than the question: Did the customer get an answer to the question? Other aspects could include speed of response, customer service courtesy, time the customer had to spend on Hold, and whether or not internal employees were adequately trained. In other words, the study of the hypothesis often demonstrates that in order to solve the problem, we also have to identify it completely, and not just settle for the most apparent symptom of that problem.

We have another opportunity to ensure excellence in the "expectations" phase. If we expect the customer to (1) get an answer on the first contact, (2) spend as little time as possible on Hold, (3) speak to a fully trained, knowledgeable, and friendly employee, and (4) come away from the experience feeling satisfied, then we have identified a set of expectations.

Finally, we test the improved system. One way, for example, would be to pose as a customer, make a phone call, and experience the customer service treatment firsthand. This is not only efficient, it is also more reliable than other methods like customer surveys. In a retail environment, we can visit a store to witness how customers are treated; in a service environment, we depend on the telephone, e-mail, and other indirect contact; and when products or services are sold primarily online, we need to have easy access to web sites, including easy-to-find contact information, tracking of inquiries, and other desirable features.

A CUSTOMER'S PERSPECTIVE

The scientific method brings order to the project. All projects have to begin with *definition* and without that first step, we cannot know how to proceed. If we do not understand the problem, we cannot fix it. It is often the case that, in the desire to rush to a solution, many projects begin without proper definition. Solutions are not always neat or simple; at times, for example, a problem manifested in a single department is the result of layer upon layer of contributing problems from other places. To truly define the problem, we need to examine it using the scientific method, accepting the possibility that the problem involves far more than what is immediately apparent and will require more work than we estimated at the beginning. If we settle for the easy fix, then we probably will not be able to truly fix the problem at all. "For every human problem, there is a neat, plain solution—and it is always wrong."[2]

We need to define customer requirements and expectations as part of the initial phase in a Six Sigma project. In fact, by emphasizing the service-related questions, we arrive at a better understanding of what needs to be fixed. Another aspect of the defining process is to determine what customer requirements and expectations are *not* being met today. We should not limit our definitions to what we believe today's system could provide more quickly or more cheaply. In fact, a better question to ask is: Does the customer require or expect something that we are not providing?

If the analysis is going to be limited to today's process, you will not know what is lacking. So a finely-run project may, in fact, address only a symptom and not the underlying problem itself. For example, if your Customer Service Department does not always provide answers because employees are not well trained, what is the solution? Better training will address that particular problem, so on the surface this may be one of those neat, plain solutions. But the real problems may be far deeper. Perhaps customers are frustrated because they have to spend a long time on Hold; they are directed to the wrong department; and employees often do not respond directly to what they are saying. These problems are far more serious than lack of training; in fact, they may accelerate customer dissatisfaction. So part of the solution may be to identify ways that the question What is not being provided? can be answered.

Key Point The popular way to study customer service is to begin with the question: How are we doing? This does not address the most common flaw in service; the right question should be: What are we *not* doing that we should be doing?

How do you find out what is not being offered today? Surveys are not going to reveal much, and isolated studies that involve little or no customer contact are not practical. The fastest way to find out what is wrong is to go through the experience yourself. Call your own customer service telephone number and make notes about the experience. To expand your range of research, also call a competitor. What do they do better? How could your system be changed to provide better service than the competitor's?

These defining steps are good beginnings for a Six Sigma project. Place your emphasis on definition at the very beginning, to avoid spending the time and energy of your team in fixing only a small portion of the problem. Listen to the *voice of the customer* (*VOC*).

Gathering information for the VOC does not have to be formalized or complex. The degree of information-gathering should depend more on the nature of the project, the people or departments involved, and the complexity of the problem itself. A central question in the VOC analysis should be: How well do we understand the customer's requirements and expectations? If

Voice of the Customer (VOC) in Six Sigma analysis, information gained by observation of a customer's requirements and expectations; the true needs of the customer, as opposed to the assumed needs under which the company operates.

you ask this question of most people, they are likely to tell you that they understand their customers quite well. Upon analysis, however, we may find that we really do *not* understand the customer at all. For example, if your company sells a product, then one attitude may be that "customer service works as long as products are shipped quickly." In fact, though, even external customers have service requirements beyond completion of orders. They expect follow-up information, technical support, warranty work, training, and more—after-sale service, in fact, often determines the difference in the consumer's mind between "excellent service" and "poor service." Given the possibility that two competitors sell products essentially identical in terms of cost and quality, the real differences are going to become apparent in nonproduct support services. This is where a lot of problems arise, and should be a primary emphasis in any project whose intention it is to improve customer service. The VOC will tell you that this is the most important area for concern.

In identifying the VOC for the purpose of improving customer service, you will need to overcome resistance in many forms:

- ✔ Opinions internally that "we already know what the customer wants."
- ✔ The assumption that service levels are already acceptable, "or we would have heard from the customer by now."
- ✔ Complete unawareness of the need to improve, or worse, lack of concern because the customer has no choice; "where else are they going to go?" is a destructive attitude, but far too common.
- ✔ The belief that "customer service" is a waste of time and money.

All of these forms of resistance are misguided and successful service-oriented projects have proven over and over that (1) many companies do not know what the customer wants, (2) customers who are dissatisfied do not usually let you know, (3) everyone benefits when you improve what you offer, and (4) improved service projects save a significant amount of time and money. Six Sigma is a profit center in this regard; projects not only pay for themselves, they also generate revenues through improved service at all levels, external and internal.

The VOC is not a one-time effort made at the defining phase of a Six Sigma process. In fact, it should be a process that you go through continually. Understanding customer requirements and expectations should be part of your job, and this applies to every employee in the organization. Just as many people do not really understand what the customer wants, we also are likely to discover that we do not really know who our customer is at all. Asking the question—the answer to which may seem obvious—can help many people revise their basic assumptions about how to relate to that customer.

Example: In a master insurance agency, a lot of process emphasis was put on the development of product literature and support for field offices. In the minds of many employees, the "customer" was the person who bought insurance policies. In fact, however, it was the insurance agent working in the field office whose requirements and expectations really mattered. This awareness of the salesperson—who had usually been perceived as pushy, demanding, constantly complaining—was not just a loud voice interfering with home office processes. In fact, these folks were the customers.

Once you know who the customer is and what that customer wants, you will be able to develop internal performance standards. What would you consider "minimum" service and "excellent" service levels? Internally, does the Accounting Department consider it important to deliver checks to salespeople in a timely manner? Or is their emphasis on account coding, balancing budgets, and complying with internal audit standards? By defining performance standards, an accountant who is preoccupied with the process-related demands of the job may become aware of the *customer*, perhaps for the first time.

Key Point We need to re-focus the emphasis in our thinking, away from details and processes, toward a definition of performance standards—with service in mind.

This flaw in thinking is not the employee's fault. It is business as usual, and commonly held opinions and attitudes are difficult to change, at least using traditional quality control methods. Under those methods, emphasis is placed on reducing costs and on service for the external customer only. Few corporations recognize the need for improved customer service in the administrative offices of the company, but once that change takes place, the entire culture of the organization may change dramatically. This is the goal under the Six Sigma program.

MANAGEMENT'S ROLE AND PARTICIPATION

Whether your Six Sigma process involves an external customer or an internal customer, the purpose of the program is the same: to improve levels of service to define and then to *meet* customer requirements and expectations.

Everyone will speculate, of course, about how Six Sigma will actually work. Will the corporate culture really change? Will this change improve morale? The effectiveness of Six Sigma depends on how committed management is to the program. This does not mean merely tolerating the existence of the program or requiring divisions and departments to figure out how it all works. Management—all the way to the top—has to be a part of the Six Sigma culture, by not only supporting the concepts but through active participation. So many quality programs emphasize technical and process improvements. Very technical processes do benefit from in-depth analysis of machinery, efficiency, and other aspects of a broad quality program. But Six Sigma is also involved with improving the work environment for all employees. To that end, top management must be involved in order for the larger, cultural change to work.

Management determines, for example, what is actually done with the information you gain from your Six Sigma project. For example, if you identify a method for process of work that improves service levels without increasing costs or expenses, the obvious reaction is to implement your recommendations. But if your CEO has given only lip service to the whole concept of quality, then the CEO's involvement is nonexistent. Six Sigma and the ideals of a changed corporate culture are viewed only as a "vision thing."[3]

What you do with the information you gain from the Six Sigma process is going to depend largely on the dedication of the company's leadership to the whole concept. Management has two roles in Six Sigma. First is overall support and participation, the philosophy that allows Six Sigma to thrive. Second is the development of strategic benefits and tactics—in other words, the process by which information is developed and passed through the process, from origination to final outcome. In Chapter 6, we apply this principle in the development of a horizontal process flowchart. The process of identifying how work moves through is also known as the *value chain*, a term used to describe the activities required to effectively design and deliver the necessary final result, or outcome.[4]

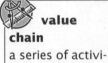 **value chain** a series of activities required to effectively design, market, and deliver a product, service, or other outcome.

Why is it management's job to lead the effort in defining quality? In fact, it is management's primary leadership role to define methods that improve the quality of a company's service and product, at all levels. Management sets the tone. If your executive leadership does not want to be involved with the daily details of creating quality, then they have no right to expect anyone else to adopt the right attitude. Management has to lead by example, as the saying goes. This is a thankless task in the traditional interactions of corporate culture, where resistance to any new ideas can prevent and sabotage the best of intentions. Six Sigma enables such change while providing the tools to management to *lead* the corporation out of the traditional rut and into a more enlightened, success-oriented quality method of thinking.

The traditional corporate culture, in which management by example is the most difficult mode of operation, makes *change* itself a difficult process. No one wants change under the traditional mode, in which self-interest is institutionalized. There remain few heroes in that environment. As one author wisely observed: "A perfect example of Management by Example and inspirational leadership, Joan of Arc, was rewarded for her heroism by being burned at the stake."[5]

The new, more enlightened approach to management is based on leading the entire corporation into a changed environment. Management establishes a new set of priorities, all based on the idea of improved quality. When management begins making its list, it becomes easy to prioritize those quality issues; identify likely logjams in the system (*weak links* represented by time delays, inefficiency, and other breakdowns in the process that directly harm quality); and provide managers and employees with a clear vision of how those problems need to be corrected and of how a new approach—one based on quality as a top priority—can be put into effect.

weak links
the specific points in a process where defects are most likely to occur, commonly points where a process passes from one area to another; where logjams occur; or where decisions have to be made.

Key Point   Management is supposed to lead, not just delegate. By establishing priorities based on quality, management takes a big step toward improving all processes performed in the company, and at all levels.

One of management's roles in this changed point of view, involves identifying *efficiency* in work processes. Many experts have tried to identify methods for improving employee efficiency. The corporate efficiency expert (who is neither involved with efficiency in a real sense, nor an expert) will study time required to complete tasks, often down to the second. The alleged value in such analysis is based on emphasis on process itself. It does nothing to change or fix work flow problems.

In a study of the Six Sigma approach, in which we seek to reconcile current process steps with the larger goal of creating better quality in outcome, we find many ways to improve efficiency itself. If the purpose in improving efficiency is simply to cut down the cost of processing information, products, or services, it will fail. There must be more. With *quality* as the overall interest in the study of efficiency, employees find themselves thinking in efficient terms. Quality itself is usually the result of efficient thinking. When management recognizes this relationship, they can lead corporate thinking into more efficient modes. People begin to see various ways in which they can achieve better quality through improvements in their own process efficiency. This is where the efficiency expert fails. By emphasizing the cost of process rather than critically evaluating how processes can be changed and improved, the expert misses the point.

One revelation that most people come upon when thinking in quality mode is that the single most important aspect of efficiency is the level of work in process. In a manufacturing environment, this means "goods in the process of being produced from raw materials through to finished goods." Of course, the more volume of work in process, the less efficiently work can be performed. This manufacturing concept applies to all processes. For example, a Shipping and Receiving Department is going to be less efficient when its work load is excessive, because "work in process" takes up time, and the more time spent not delivering the final result of the process, the less quality there is in the entire matter, from beginning to end.

So the question becomes: How do I reduce work in process to improve efficiency? So rather than trying to figure out how to speed up a flawed process, we get to the point of controlling work flow itself. The result—greater efficiency and, of course, higher quality—translates to lowered processing costs, improved customer satisfaction, and improved employee morale.

Management's role in Six Sigma, in a broad sense, is not limited to merely supporting the concept or even to taking part. Management needs to set the tone for a new corporate culture, one in which each and every employee begins asking a new series of questions:

✔ How do I reduce work process in my area of responsibility?

✔ What does the customer require and expect? Am I delivering that?

✔ Who, in fact, *is* my customer?

✔ What can I do next to continue improving this process?

SIX SIGMA: THEORY AND PRACTICE

Any organization attempting to change the basis of work process, is going to face some resistance. To a degree, we can define "quality" in terms of complexity. So the more complex the processes within the company, the more difficult it becomes to identify methods for upgrading output. For this reason, the formality that is possible under a Six Sigma program is valuable. Remember, it is not necessary to always use the most complex forms; but for the most complex projects, that formality is valuable. When numerous departments and people are going to play a part in a process, the greater levels of formality are indispensable; and when the decisions about making changes cross departmental lines, support from top management is essential. Many excellent ideas have simply died because a department supervisor or manager felt threatened by the change, was not consulted, or believed it reduced his or her power.

Key Point   Breaking down barriers is the key to improving process quality. Traditional systems are often used to reinforce them, to make the walls thicker and higher and, ultimately, to prevent making any changes whatsoever.

In a very real sense, the complexity of human interaction is far more complex than the complexities involved with projects. That human aspect, even in the most simple projects, is a volatile area in any company. In the traditional departmental thinking of the corporate culture, the empire-building between departments and divisions did more to prevent progress, curtail quality, and harm growth, than any capital or other resource limitations.

Example: The CEO assigned a manager the task of proposing a revised floor plan for the company. With growth, departments had outgrown their areas and employees for some areas were scattered about. The *intention* of this project was to devise a means for organizing the departments more efficiently.

The outcome, in spite of good intentions, was to cause tremendous upset and anger among virtually all the department managers in the company. Complaints included:

- ✔ *Exclusion:* A manager was angry that his opinion had not been sought prior to drawing up a proposed revision plan.
- ✔ *Loss of power:* One manager measured current versus proposed office space and concluded that the plan would deprive her of about 20 square feet.
- ✔ *Change:* Several people resisted the plan because it meant moving people around.

The complexity of the human aspect of this fairly simple proposal grew from the fact that there had been no communication beforehand. In a Six Sigma approach to the same issue, the team would have started by articulating the *problem*—inefficiency in the floor plan that arose from employee growth. Next, they would have asked department managers for ideas. Finally, any plan would have been identified as a preliminary and proposed solution, as one of many ways that people and departments could be shuffled around. The original, traditional approach was done the way it was partly to avoid costly rewiring of the internal telephone system. Such minor considerations may cause great trouble elsewhere; but again, this was a traditional approach to solving a problem; it did not consider the larger picture, including the likely response to managers who felt left out of the process itself.

If we consider all department managers as "customers" of the manager assigned to revise the floor plan—

even just as a sketch on one possible idea—what was the cause of the negative response? The primary problem with the approach was a "service vacuum," the range of problems that arose from a lack of communication. Virtually all the responses could have been eliminated with a single process of definition, coupled with a request for suggestions.

The input from various department managers certainly would not have helped to arrive at a solution that would be universally acceptable to everyone. However, the purpose to any project, under Six Sigma or any other method, is not to achieve consensus; the democratic ideal is not an efficient model. The purpose to a Six Sigma process is to gather information so that the entire scope of a problem may be better understood; and to then develop solutions that address the entire range of issues so that most of them are addressed adequately.

For example, asking managers to propose solutions is not merely a means for avoiding anger from managers. It is a useful process designed to better identify the problem. After the sketch had been proposed to the CEO, several managers' concerns came to light. Has those concerns been known ahead of time, the plan itself would have been much different—and better—because the whole range of departmental placement was more complex than the initial definition of the problem. Under that definition, the solitary goal was to get all the employees reporting to one manager in the same floor space area. The manager doing the project restricted his possible design level by also considering current telephone exchange locations. However, there were other considerations not known in advance. These included:

✔ The Supply Department needed close access to the freight elevator at the rear of the building, but the proposed design moved the department to the middle floor area, which was simply not practical.

✔ Three specialized sub-departments involved in accounting routines had originally been placed next to the main accounting area. Under the revised plan, the departments were scattered around the floor. The manager doing the design work was not aware of the need for these areas to be situated close to one another.

✔ One department handled customer cash and, by regulation, was required to be set apart from other departments in what was called a "cage" area. The proposed redesign called for moving this department out of the cage area and, in fact, dismantling the cage itself. The manager designing the revised floor plan was not aware of the regulatory requirement.

You would not move Shipping and Receiving to the penthouse or anywhere else far away from the loading dock. But that requirement is visible. Many requirements are not visible to an outsider. This points out the absolute requirements for careful definition of the *range* of issues involved in process quality; participation by all of those involved; and the crafting of solutions that take into account the visible *and* invisible requirements for each participant.

Key Point Analysis, for all the value it provides, is only as good as the input you receive from those involved in the process. Analysis without information is quite useless.

The example points out the value of Six Sigma. Most quality programs are focused on the idea of how processes can be done more cheaply or more quickly. The bottom line is at the heart of such programs. Six Sigma serves as an analytical tool as well as a quality program. So the corporate culture, when modified to be based on participation and service as essential elements for all processes, makes it work. The *theory* of Six Sigma works in practice as well, because it is designed to be much more than just the exercise of changing processes to cut costs and make everything faster.

While reducing costs and improving process efficiency, Six Sigma requires that we identify ways to reduce complexity. Processes tend to become overly complex. One person proposes a change for a specific reason, and that change becomes permanent. A later fix, proposed by someone else, may not consider the practical aspects of the big picture, or its effect on other departments. For example, in one company someone proposed preparing job requisitions in five parts instead of in three parts. The purpose: to provide follow-up documentation for back orders (copy # 4) and to allow the CEO to track ordering trends (copy # 5).

These requirements came about for two reasons. First, about 10 percent of orders had to be back ordered and the company had not developed a reliable follow-up procedure. Second, the CEO was in the habit of borrowing accounting copies of requisitions, using them to study trends, and not returning them; it caused a lot of chaos.

However, setting a policy to create two additional pieces of paper for all orders was not efficient. It added to the cost of routing orders, the printing of order forms, filing and storage, and—in the final analysis—it did not solve the problems. There remained no efficient or reliable method for following up on back orders because no one used the extra copy to put any working processes into effect. And the CEO continued using the accounting copy, explaining that they were easier to read. Copy # 5 was so light it was difficult to read, so the CEO preferred going to the originals.

Six Sigma solved the problems created by non-solutions like the ones in the example, by requiring a five-step approach. This approach reduces complexity while resulting in effective and realistic improvements in processes:

1. *Analysis and evaluation.* All projects have to begin with this step. No matter how simple a problem appears at first, it is invariably more complex than anyone thinks.

2. *Standardization.* Simplicity of choice translates to less work in process, easier training curve, and lower costs for everyone. If you need extra copies of a document for only 10 percent of cases, it is not necessary to design a new form and create a new paper trail for 100 percent. By standardizing processes and dealing with exceptions in *exceptional* ways, you preserve the efficiency of a well-designed process.

3. *Cross-process efficiency.* The problems of duplication in effort, conflicts in responsibility, and uncertainty about tasking contribute to the chaos so often experienced in internal processing. Lines have to be drawn clearly so that everyone who takes part in a specific routine understands the three process elements, which can be expressed in the three questions: What starts the task? (Or where do I get the information, materials, or requests?) What am I supposed to do, and what is the deadline? (Or how do I process and when does someone else expect the outcome?) And third, What do I do with the results? (Or where do I send it next?) The ability to articulate the process steps for each participant is at the heart of creating, maintaining, and ensuring ongoing quality. (See Chapter 6 for an example of how these forms of efficiency can be summarized using the horizontal flowchart.)

4. *Cross-departmental cooperation.* This is the most challenging part of a quality control program under traditional methods. Remember, those methods are based on the assumption that departments are working models unto themselves, by definition isolated, and by desire not to be invaded by other departments. So if Shipping and Receiving is unable to ship orders within three days, that is *their* problem and *they* have to solve it. The fact that the problem is created elsewhere does not enter into the equation because, putting it bluntly, in the traditional corporate culture, departments do not cooperate with one another. This prevents process improvement and harms quality; it makes the permanent success of any quality program impossible because it is designed to fail. In the traditional approach to quality, only a small minority of problems—those within the exclusive control of a single department—can be solved.

5. *Follow-up.* One thing that all quality programs share is the need to follow up after changes have been made. Most people realize that success does not just happen; it has to be monitored, cajoled, encouraged, begged, and modified—in other words, even the most successful

Six Sigma project does not end with the final recommendation and implementation; it has to be followed up to ensure that it is continuing to work.

The methods for reducing complexity fit well in a comprehensive Six Sigma program. In the next chapter, we examine two important sub-methodologies of Six Sigma: systems called DMAIC (define, measure, analyze, improve, and control) and DMADV (define, measure, analyze, design, and verify).

Chapter 4

The Nature of Quality

I had been on Hold for several minutes when the customer service clerk returned. My question was a simple one: "Why can't I open my credit card statement online?" The clerk mumbled something about trying again, and I told her I had been trying for more than a week. "Well maybe there's a problem," she said. "Can you write us a letter explaining what you need?" I asked whether a supervisor was available, and she replied, "I'm the supervisor."

If we are to provide *quality* service, we have to ask ourselves exactly how we will go about doing that. Putting poorly trained employees on a telephone and expecting them to field customer inquiries is not enough. In fact, that may only make matters worse, because we compound a problem by adding frustration on top of it.

THE TACTICS OF QUALITY

Six Sigma is originated from the strategic design that management creates. Once that design is passed through the organization, the *tactics* to be employed are developed at the team level and put into action. In this chapter we explain the tactical elements of the Six Sigma project, using a system called *DMAIC* (define, measure, analyze, improve, control).

 DMAIC
the tactical approach to Six Sigma projects, involving five phases: define, measure, analyze, improve and control.

The whole process begins when management identifies top priorities of the entire Six Sigma program. These highest-priority projects should reflect what management considers the most urgent concerns: drains on cash flow and profits, inefficient processes, ineffective internal controls, lack of coordination between marketing and administrative sections, and declining market share. So the strategic importance of Six Sigma will touch upon many areas and ultimately is likely to impact every employee in the company. The dual purpose of Six Sigma—improving the methodology of quality improvement, while also changing the whole corporate culture—relies on the use of predictable and formal tactical programs. This is where DMAIC comes into play.

Key Point   The strategic definition of Six Sigma leads to the action plan, which is articulated in the tactical phases of DMAIC.

In the desire to create a work environment with improved effectiveness and efficiency, we have to contend with a number of realities: the political power struggles that exist between departments and sections, the natural resistance to change, cynicism about quality control in general, and the high-stress demands of organizational life in which deadlines and emergencies are constantly looming.

Employing the specific tactics of Six Sigma is a method of bringing order and certainty to the chaotic and stressful environment of the workplace. It is not a simple task. Just as management has a formidable job in designing a new cultural approach to work process itself, the Six Sigma team needs to overcome the day-to-day barriers to change and new assignments, before Six Sigma can begin to work well. The most common response to the news that someone is expected to take part on a quality control team is that they are already too busy to take on the added burden. This resistance can be overcome by explaining that their role is not going to be time-consuming because other members of the team will share the time burden. Once employees come to realize that Six Sigma is a serious program and management wants to implement it, the usual forms of resistance will probably dissipate.

A few steps that can be taken at middle management levels will help to reduce resistance. No one wants to be on a team in which the team leader dictates all the processes and then takes all the credit for the team's success. So while Six Sigma processes should assign greater responsibilities to middle management, it should also ensure that recognition is shared by the entire team. One tendency in quality team definition is to make the mistake of creating large groups to tackle problems. If a problem is especially complex, it makes more sense to focus on smaller team groupings with better interaction, contact, and opportunities to work together. Larger groups, by definition, are not as effective as smaller groups. A complex project does not have to be tackled all at once and can be broken down into phases, with different teams involved in highly specialized areas. The efforts of several teams are then coordinated by the leadership of the Six Sigma organization working with the various sponsors overseeing multiple teams.

If we recall that one central purpose is to improve processes and, thus, improve overall quality, we can structure the tactical approach with several specific goals in mind. These vary with the exact nature of each project. Goals may include cutting time required to complete processes, changing the process to better meet the customer's requirements and expectations, improving the process monitoring system, and reducing the costs of the process.

GETTING FROM CONCEPT TO QUALITY

In all phases of developing the Six Sigma program, we should remember to continually be aware of the customer's point of view. The tactics of Six Sigma are process-oriented so it is easy to lose sight of the end purpose in the work itself.

Little things make a big difference. From the customer's point of view, a step as simple as a follow-up telephone call to ask whether the customer was satisfied with the transaction is both refreshing and personal. Imagine applying the same standards to fellow employees, vendors, or the regulators who audit our books. It is so rare for a customer service mentality to be applied outside the direct sales contact, that when it does exist, everyone is surprised. However, it makes perfect sense.

By the same argument, little *negative* things also make a big difference. For example, the tone of signs in a store can impress customers negatively. YOU MUST HAVE YOUR RECEIPT posted at a return desk is authoritarian. An alternative that is somewhat softer in tone makes a lot of difference. PLEASE HAVE RECEIPTS READY is easier to digest and, incidentally, should not necessarily dictate a hard and fast policy. Many stores will allow customers to return merchandise even if they have lost their receipts. The concept that you simply cannot get your money back because you have lost a slip of paper is a punitive and unreasonable policy. These subtle policy matters make a big difference to customers.

Key Point We need to get beyond traditional definitions of "quality" and recognize that the person on the other side of the transaction sees quality far differently from the way you do. And both of you are right.

The idea of "quality" is not the same for the customer as it is for the employee. For example, the employee may see the issue as one of needing a receipt to document the transaction; the customer simply wants his or her money back and has shown up at the store with the merchandise. If a Customer Service Department operates by telephone, staffing shortages mean that customers have to wait on Hold, especially during peak hours. To the customer, however, this creates the impression that the company does not consider service a high priority.

So the actual methods employed in a Customer Service Department (or in an internal department for that matter) define *quality* from the customer's point of view. If your Accounting Department is willing and able to get your reimbursement check within a day or two (even though that creates batching exceptions), you will consider it exceptional quality. But if you have to wait two weeks because your request hit at the wrong moment in the cycle, then you will conclude that the department does not care about your requirements or expectations. From your point of view, quality of service is poor. From the Accounting Department's side, however, the twice-monthly batching system works quite well, so they are providing "excellent" service. The definitions are different. To the Accounting Department, excellence means that everything moves along smoothly, work is done on time, and employees are not wasting time on exceptions.

If we take these distinctions and apply them to every instance where you interact with another person (end user/customer, fellow employee, manager or subordinate, or auditor), you realize that several important bottom-line issues have to be considered in a tactical approach to quality:

✔ Your customer does not share your priorities. They may be quite different.

✔ The way that you define "quality" determines how the customer reacts. If quality is aimed at improving *your* process, it may ignore the requirements and expectations of *their* process experience. So, for example, a Customer Response Department may successfully cut its operating budget by reducing the number of employees on staff, but all the customer knows is that they are left on Hold for a long time.

✔ Processes are the means for delivering end results (product, service, response to inquiries, follow-up work). But processes are not end results themselves. For example, the efficiency of an Accounting Department's batch processing system is not an end result, and in fact the rigidity of that process may adversely affect perceptions about the department. By the same argument, your company may be able to get products in the mail to customers within 24 hours from day of order, but if the wrong items are being shipped, the process is flawed to the extent that the end result—delivery of the product—is also flawed. Timely delivery is not sufficient if the wrong item is in the box.

There are five specific phases in the Six Sigma tactical application. These are collectively referred to as DMAIC (define, measure, analyze, improve, control). This tactical system is the core of Six Sigma, and following its sequence determines the success of each Six Sigma project.

The working sequence and checkpoints of DMAIC are summarized in the process map shown in Figure 4.1.

Note that in moving forward to the *measure* phase, the team may discover that it is necessary to return to *define* and make modifications. The same methodical step occurs from the *analyze* phase back to the *measure* phase and again from *improve* to *analyze*. In the *analyze* phase, the team may also discover that it is necessary to return to the *define* stage and restate part of the initial assumptions of the project.

Key Point   The process of performing, evaluating, and going back ensures that the Six Sigma tactical process is complete and focused. The same interim checking applies to process work flow itself and dramatically reduces defects.

Is this a lot of busy work and time wasting? We have all seen the flowchart analysis with work loops, in which we continually refer back to fix errors or inch forward; the concepts often are well intended but simply do not work. However, in Six Sigma, this exacting approach is designed to ensure that (1) everyone understands the purpose of the project, (2) the team has the opportunity to modify the initial definitions upon discovery of important facts, and (3) by the time the *improve* and *control phases* are implemented, the complete problem has been addressed. Nothing is as disheartening as finding out that a project

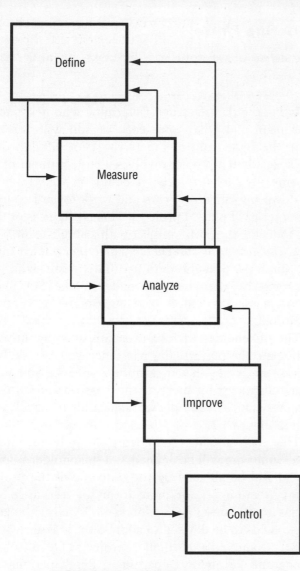

FIGURE 4.1 DMAIC process map.

has been extremely successful in fixing a problem only to then discover that in fact, the problem that was fixed was only one segment of a much larger problem.

The purpose of the different stages is to enable the team to move through the process knowing that it has taken all the right steps in the right order.

The Define *Phase*

In the *define* phase, four specific tasks are undertaken. These are:

1. *Put together the team.* Determine who needs to be on the team and what roles each person will perform. Picking the right team members can be a difficult decision, especially if a project involves a large number of departments. In such projects, it could be wise to break them down into smaller pieces and work toward completion of a series of phased projects. This is often easier than trying to tackle the entire project with a single team.

2. *Document the stakeholders and undertake a stakeholder analysis.* Stakeholders are individuals who will be affected by the changes made in the Six Sigma process—managers, employees, customers, or vendors, for example.

stakeholder analysis
a process in which the project team determines who will be affected by the outcome of a Six Sigma project.

The stakeholder analysis is usually a listing intended to anticipate the players, the resistance you are likely to run into, the issues that determine resistance and interests, and a strategy for meeting those issues and for overcoming resistance. A sample worksheet for this analysis is shown in Figure 4.2.

This is a worksheet intended to help the team identify everyone who will be defined as a stakeholder—someone who will be affected by the outcome of the project, who may exhibit one or more forms of resistance, and who has real issues to be addressed. Finally, a specific strategy needs to be devised to address those issues.

For example, a particular project may affect the Shipping and Receiving Department. Resistance may include concern that changing the current system will add time to the processing of both incoming and outgoing items. The real issue, however, might be concern about the timing of deliveries. There is a tendency for departments to show up toward the shipping deadline with large numbers of packages; these all need to be processed immediately, and it causes chaos in the department. So in developing a specific strategy, the team would need to

Stakeholder	Resistance	Issues	Strategies

FIGURE 4.2 Stakeholder analysis worksheet.

understand both the reason for resistance and the real underlying issues that cause it.

3. *Develop a project charter.* This is a document that names the project, summarizes the project by explaining the *business case* in a brief statement, and lists the project scope and goals.

A form for the project charter is provided in Figure 4.3.

project charter
a document summarizing the important elements of the project: name, business case, scope and goals.

Project Charter for _____

Business Case _____
_____

Project Scope _____
_____
_____

Project Goals _____
_____
_____
_____

Notes _____
_____
_____
_____

Special Requirements _____
_____
_____
_____

FIGURE 4.3 Project charter worksheet.

The worksheet is used to document the underlying assumptions of the project, what it is intended to achieve, and its scope.

4. *Develop the SIPOC process map.* This is a flowchart documenting process steps, which also lists out the Suppliers, Inputs, Process, Output, and Customer. This is a highly detailed requirement and Chapter 6 provides a sample of how this is organized and prepared. A "Supplier" may be an outside vendor or another department, just as a "Customer" can appear in many forms.

The SIPOC process map is essential for identifying (1) the way processes occur currently and (2) how those processes should be modified and improved throughout the remaining phases of DMAIC.

Some Six Sigma *define* phases are by necessity more heavily involved in documenting and discussing details of the project. These are not always essential. The design of the process should be determined by the scope of the project and the need to ensure that the whole team is on the same level of understanding about its elements. In more advanced applications, these phases of the *define* phase would include:

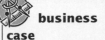

business case
a summary of the purpose to the project, its financial impact, and the problem the team intends to address.

SIPOC
a process map that identifies all the elements of a project: Suppliers, Input, Process, Output, and Customers.

✔ Definition of the "customer" along with expectations and requirements.

✔ Diagrams meant to improve understanding by all team members of the project's purpose.

✔ Critical-to-quality (CTQ) tree, a device that translates customer needs into product and service action points. In Chapter 6, we demonstrate how CTQ can be incorporated into the horizontal process diagram (SIPOC).

Key Point Design should itself be structured based on the complexity of the project. A flexible design is crucial because every project is different.

At the conclusion of the *design* phase, you should know who the customer or end user is, their resistance, issues, and requirements. You should also have a clear understanding of goals and the scope of the project (including budget, time constraints, deadlines).

The *Measure* Phase

There are three parts to the *measure* phase. These are:

1. *Data collection.* The reason to collect data is to identify areas where current processes need to be improved. You collect data from three primary sources: input, process, and output. The input source is where the process is generated. For example, a sales rep delivers orders to the Marketing Department. That is one form of input. Process data refers to tests of efficiency: the time requirements, cost, value, defects or errors, and labor spent on the process. Output is a measurement of efficiency.

2. *Data evaluation.* To evaluate how a process is working, you will want to next arrive at the current baseline Sigma. To do this, you need to calculate the approximate number of defects. That is divided by the sum of units multiplied by the number of opportunities. The sum of this calculation is then multiplied by one million to find Sigma.

Example: To show how this works, let us use an internal procedure. The measurement is made of the problem involving packages that are supposed to be sent within three days from the date an order is placed. Your data collection reveals the following: In one month customer orders were handled by three departments (number of opportunities) and a total of 426 customer orders (units) were processed. In studying the space between order date and shipment date, you discover that 94 orders were shipping out later than three days from the date of the order. Base Sigma is calculated using this information:

$$\frac{94}{426 \times 3} \times 1,000,000 = 73,552$$

We expand the summarized Sigma chart from Chapter 1 to show the next step. This detailed chart is shown in Table 4.1.

In finding the defects per million on this chart, we see that 73,552 is just below a Sigma of 2.9. Now we have a quantified quality level. With the goal being improving the Sigma level, when we reduce defects, we would expect to see an improvement as a result, and it will be measurable. In the preceding example, we estimated that there were three opportunities because three departments handled orders; and that there were 426 units processed during a month. In that time, we experienced 94 defects. This means that 94 packages were not shipped within three days.

The project aimed at making this process work better would examine procedures in the sales rep's handling of orders; in the Marketing Department; and in Shipping and Receiving. If it were possible to cut the number of defects in half, Sigma would be improved to:

$$\frac{47}{426 \times 3} \times 1,000,000 = 36,776$$

According to the chart in Table 4.1, the Sigma would then be about 3.3. While this would be a substantial improvement, we would still be experiencing 47 defects, a number far too high.

This is the method used for measuring results as we proceed through a project. This beginning point enables us to locate the cause and effect of those processes and to seek defect point so that the procedure can be improved.

3. *FMEA (Failure Mode and Effects Analysis).* The final segment of the *measure* phase is called FMEA. This is a fancy engineering term that refers to preventing defects before they occur. It helps you to define exactly what can go wrong.

The FMEA process usually includes rating possible defects, or failures, in three ways: the likelihood that something will go wrong, the ability to detect a defect, and the level of severity of the defect. You may use a rating scale. For example, rate each of these three areas from

> **FMEA (Failure Mode and Effects Analysis)**
> A process for identifying likely defects before they occur, using a rating scale; the purpose is to identify areas where preventive measures will be useful in a process.

TABLE 4.1 Sigma Table					
Sigma	Defects per Million	Yield	Sigma	Defects per Million	Yield
6.0	3	99.9997%	3.0	66,807	93.3
5.9	5	99.99946	2.9	80,757	91.9
5.8	9	99.99915	2.8	96,801	90.3
5.7	13	99.9987	2.7	115,070	88.5
5.6	21	99.9979	2.6	135,666	86.4
5.5	32	99.9968	2.5	158,655	84.1
5.4	48	99.995	2.4	184,060	81.6
5.3	72	99.993	2.3	211,855	78.8
5.2	108	99.989	2.2	241,964	75.8
5.1	159	99.985	2.1	274,253	72.6
5.0	233	99.98	2.0	308,538	69.1
4.9	337	99.97	1.9	344,578	65.5
4.8	483	99.95	1.8	382,089	61.8
4.7	687	99.93	1.7	420,740	57.9
4.6	968	99.9	1.6	460,172	54.0
4.5	1,350	99.87	1.5	500,000	50.0
4.4	1,866	99.81	1.4	539,828	46.0
4.3	2,555	99.74	1.3	579,260	42.1
4.2	3,467	99.65	1.2	617,911	38.2
4.1	4,661	99.5	1.1	655,422	34.5
4.0	6,210	99.4	1.0	691,462	30.9
3.9	8,198	99.2	0.9	725,747	27.4
3.8	10,724	98.9	0.8	758,036	24.2
3.7	13,903	98.6	0.7	788,145	21.2
3.6	17,864	98.2	0.6	815,940	18.4
3.5	22,750	97.7	0.5	841,345	15.9
3.4	28,716	97.1	0.4	864,334	13.6
3.3	35,930	96.4	0.3	884,930	11.5
3.2	44,565	95.5	0.2	903,199	9.7
3.1	54,799	94.5	0.1	919,243	8.1
			0.0	933,193	6.7

1 to 10, with 1 being the lowest FMEA level and 10 being the highest. The higher the level, the more severe the rating. So a high FMEA would indicate the need to devise and implement improved measuring steps within the overall process. This would have the effect of preventing defects. Clearly, there is no need to spend a lot of time on this procedure if the likelihood of a defect is low; because this procedure is a form of process-specific internal control, its value is greatest when the likelihood of a defect is high.

Key Point By rating anticipated defects, we develop a sense of how effectively the controls of the Six Sigma project are going to work. The rating shows us where we need to do more work.

In Chapter 6, we apply this principle in the horizontal flowchart and identify "weak links" in processes. These could also be called likely FMEA points. Knowing that the likelihood of a defect is important, of course. It is also important to know where that defect is most likely to occur. In a process involving two or more departments, the weak link—a point where the process passes from one department or person to another—is also the most likely point for a defect to occur. So being aware of the FMEA rating becomes useful when you are trying to reduce defects, because you would use the FMEA rating to concentrate on weak links.

The Analyze *Phase*

Some Six Sigma policies involve a complex array of complex mathematical formulas, diagrams, and other forms of analysis. However, the purpose of Six Sigma should be kept in mind. We want to define the causes of defects, measure those defects, and analyze them so that they can be reduced. If it is necessary or helpful to produce visual representations of the processes and defects being studied, then they are worth the time and effort. However, for most processes—as well as for most team members—a nontechnical approach will be far more effective.

If we view Six Sigma as a participatory effort, then the more people who are comfortable being involved in the format of the project, the better. This assumes that you will be able to achieve the desired result—fewer defects with greater efficiency and effectiveness—without needing to develop a series of mathematical analysis.

With this in mind, we present a non-technical version of the *analysis* phase of DMAIC. We will consider five specific types of analysis that will help to promote the goals of the project. These are source, process, data, resource, and communication analysis.

1. *Source analysis.* Also called "root cause" analysis, this procedure attempts to find defects that are derived from the sources of information or work generation. In the example of late shipment of goods from Shipping and Receiving, the problem comes from the fact that the sales rep promised delivery within three days. However, orders often are not sent to the Marketing Department immediately. A process delay occurs in Marketing frequently. And because the Accounting Department does not always pay vendors on a timely basis, the supplier providing basic shipping materials has held up delivery pending payment from last month. In this brief view of the situation, a source analysis reveals problems in Sales, Marketing, and Accounting. Those problems have to be resolved before we can expect to eliminate defects in Shipping and Receiving.

2. *Process analysis.* The source analysis is often difficult to distinguish from process analysis. The *process* refers to the precise movement of materials, information, or requests from one place to another. In the Shipping and Receiving example, we can identify the sources of problems. Now, let us further check the process itself. The fact that orders do not arrive in a timely manner is one of several potential problems. What if the inventory is not well organized and there are no products on hand, even though records show that there should be? This is an additional likely process defect that needs to be fixed.

3. *Data analysis.* The data may be flawed as well, further adding to the complexity of the problem and generating defects. What if orders do not provide all the needed information, such as the *product* to be shipped? This would add further delays because the shipping employees would have to track the order back through Marketing and Sales before they would be able to proceed. A problem in inventory records may cause unreasonably high levels of back order or even inaccuracy in the basic records.

4. *Resource analysis.* We also need to ensure that employees are properly trained in all departments that affect the process. If training is inadequate, you want to identify that as a cause of defects. Other resources include raw materials needed to manufacture, process, and deliver the goods. So if the Accounting Department is not paying vendor bills on time and, consequently, the vendor holds up a shipment of shipping supplies, this becomes a resource problem.

5. *Communication analysis.* One problem common to most processes high in defects, is poor communication. The classic interaction between a customer and a retail store is worthy of study because many of the common communication problems are apparent in this case. The same types of problems occur with the internal customer as well, even though we may not recognize the sequence of events as a customer service problem. The exercise of looking at issues from both points of view is instructive. A customer wants fast delivery, but Shipping and Receiving is more concerned with lack of basic supplies and unreliable inventory records. A vendor wants payment according to agreed-upon terms, but the Accounting Department wants to make its batch processing uniform and efficient (as defined by elimination of exceptions). The disconnect between these groups demonstrates the importance of communication analysis.

Analysis can take several forms. Some Six Sigma programs like to use a lot of diagrams and worksheets, and others prefer discussion and list making. The proper procedure is the one that works best for your team, provided that the end result is successful.

The Improve *Phase*

In many efforts to improve the way that things are done, people look for the obvious or fast fix. If goods are not being delivered on time, if merchandise is broken during shipment, or if the wrong items are being sent out, the immediate response is to look for a singular cause, and change it. The idea that the problem can be resolved instantly and without in-depth investigation is naïve but understandable. We find, over and over, that in fact, problems tend to be complex and multifaceted. We would expect to need to make improvements in many areas of the company, given the natural complexity of the majority of problems.

Key Point   Problem-solving people may want to rush to solutions. But some problems are more complex and less obvious than we would like. For this reason, the results-oriented team member may need to slow down and follow the process. It might lead somewhere interesting.

We approach the *improve* phase with these realizations in mind. In the Six Sigma project, how do we improve what we discover? This is the phase where dramatic improvement is put into action, where defect rates are eliminated, and Sigma is raised far higher than it has ever been before.

But for this to occur, we have to ensure that these improvements are made at all the process segments where defects have occurred or could occur in the future.

Improvement can involve a simple fix once we discover the causes of defects. However, in some cases, we may need to employ additional tools as well. These include:

✔ *Solution alternatives.* Some creative solutions occur in team settings. While the tendency of a group might be to overthink and thus overcomplicate the improvements needed to solve the problem, an individual might arrive at the obvious but simple answer. For example, a truck is firmly stuck under an overpass. The driver ignored the height limitations and got his rig good and stuck. Numerous police, fire, and other experts consider many ways to force the truck out of the wedge, but nothing works. A small child, a passenger in one of the many cars stuck in line behind the truck, asks one of the fire fighters, "Why don't you let the air out of the tires?" The solution, so obvious and so easy, did not occur to anyone else.

The same kinds of creative fixes apply in business settings. In Chapter 2, we give the example of a company asked to provide a lifetime warranty by one large customer, in place of the standard 10-year warranty. After many meetings where employees considered alternatives for tracking inventory with this requirement in mind, one team member suggested giving *all* customers a lifetime warranty. Since no products had ever been returned, and no complaints about breakdown had ever been received, the solution was obvious.

Another form of solution alternative comes up when two different but equally viable solutions are presented for consideration. The decision to pick one over the other may be made on the basis of time requirements and cost. However, these are not always significantly different, so this leads to the second improvement tool, experimentation.

✔ *Experiments with solution alternatives.* Testing of different solution ideas fits well with the precepts of the scientific method. If we simply do not know what will work and what will not, we need to conduct an objective experiment to find out. For example, a quality team of the U.S. Navy was given the task of figuring out how to reduce the cost of replacing copper piping in nuclear submarines. Each sub had hundreds of miles of pipe, but at each maintenance cycle, it took a long time to go through the replacement process. The team concluded that the program should abandon copper pipe altogether and begin using stainless steel. Even though the alternative material cost more, the labor savings more than made up the difference. Because stainless steel lasts far longer than copper, the solution was creative and effective. Even so, command officers were dubious so the team proposed testing the idea on a small number of subs. In an eight-month maintenance cycle, the results were obvious, so the entire program was switched over to stainless steel.[1]

✔ *Planning for future change.* Most processes are dynamic rather than stationary. So even if today's solutions are effective, we have to also allow flexibility for future change. In a rapidly growing company (or changes within a specific division or operating segment) processes may be in a constant state of change. So the *improve* phase is going to be perpetual and has to be designed to allow for additional changes in the future. To visualize this, imagine setting up a filing system manually. We know that a lot of additional files are going to be needed in the letters *E*, *M*, *S*, and *T*. So the files are set up to provide extra room for those letters.

Planning for future change is like the filing system plan, but often with many more components. So in the design of the work flow diagram (the horizontal flowchart described in Chapter 6) it is important to recognize that several points have to be incorporated into the process improvement. These include (1) flexibility for increased workload, (2) recognition that assumed deadline pressure points could be worse in the future, (3) allowance for increased defect occurrence at identified weak link points, and (4) design of the project itself for continual review and revision.

The Control *Phase*

The last phase of DMAIC is *control*, which is the phase in which we ensure that the processes continue to work well, produce desired output results, and maintain quality levels. You will be concerned with four specific aspects of control, which are:

1. *Quality control.* The ultimate purpose in control is overall assurance that a high standard of quality is met. The customer's expectations depend on this, so control is inherently associated with quality. It does little good to get shipments in the mail within three days if large numbers of them arrive broken because we did not have the time to package items correctly. It also is of no value if payroll checks are issued on time, but for all the wrong amounts. In each case the customer's expectations would not be met. Since the purpose to Six Sigma is to improve overall process by reducing defects, quality control is the essential method for keeping the whole process on track; for enabling us to spot trouble and fix it; and for judging how effectively the project was executed and implemented.

Key Point *Quality* is at the heart of the Six Sigma philosophy. Reducing defects has everything to do with striving for perfection. Whether we reach perfection or not, the effort defines our attitude toward quality itself.

2. *Standardization.* One feature of smooth processing is to enable processes to go as smoothly as possible. This usually means standardization. In a manufacturing environment, the value of standardization has been proven over and over. It is the exceptions that slow the whole process down and add costs to the output. While standardization can be damaging in and of itself (if, for example, a process does not accept exceptions under any circumstances), we need to devise a control feature to processes so that the majority of work is managed in a standardized manner. Thus, if 90 percent of purchase requisitions require an original and two copies, why should we produce a four-copy form because it may be needed 10 percent of the time?

3. *Control methods and alternatives.* The development of a new process of any change to an existing process requires the development of procedures to control work flow. In administrative departments, this usually means devising a form to track information. In a manufacturing plant, we appoint line foremen to make sure the line keeps moving and, at the same time, repetitive steps are done correctly. In any process, what happens to the exceptions? At those times when a process cannot be managed in the normal manner, we need to come up with alternatives short of forcing compliance to the standardized method. The Six Sigma team will be faced with this question and will need to develop simple but effective methods for processing both regular and exceptional work.

4. *Responding when defects occur.* The final step in a control process is knowing how to respond once a defect is discovered. The weak links in the procedure—where defects are most likely to occur—can and should be monitored carefully so that defects can be spotted and fixed before the process continues. This looping control feature makes processes most effective because in this manner defects never make it to the end of the line. The response to a defect may be to prevent a discovered flaw from becoming a defect at all. In the best designed systems, defects can be reduced to near zero, so that we may actually believe that Six Sigma can be attained.

APPLYING DMAIC

The actual attainment of Six Sigma—virtually no defects per one million opportunities—is not a realistic goal. However, when we apply DMAIC completely and superimpose it over a process, it is possible to experience a dramatic reduction in the level and occurrence of defects.

Key Point The continual checking and evaluating of work flow to ensure quality, locates emerging defects and fixes them *during* process, rather than waiting to find them at the end. The goal, of course, is to give the end checker nothing to do, because there will be no defects to fix by the time the process has been completed.

In Chapter 6, we take a relatively complex problem involving several departments, and show how DMAIC principles can be put to work to reduce defects, perhaps removing them entirely (except for the inevitable defect that does make it through even the best of systems). However, before proceeding to that point, we need to make a distinction between process and personal defects.

A *process* defect can be defined as any defect arising out of the product or service, the source of information or materials, and the nature of the customer. In a production environment, a defect would be a nonworking or incomplete unit. In a service environment, a process defect is a math error, incomplete report, upside-down page, or missed deadline. A *personal* defect can be called human error in many cases, but it is more. It may point out the problem of inadequate training, problems between shifts due to hour of the day, or defects arising from the boredom of performing repetitive work. People make mistakes due to poor training, lack of supervision, low morale, or boredom. These causes are far more intangible than tangible defects, so a Six Sigma project has to be flexible enough to recognize that the way to fix one problem is not always identical in each and every case.

Example: A Six Sigma team in a production plant was accustomed to analyzing defect trends using highly technical measurements. These included detailed charting of defect rates, as well as direct observation of production line work flow. However, one defect trend did not make sense when it first came up. The company had recently acquired a small manufacturing company and the team realized immediately that the third shift exhibited defect rates four times higher than the first two shifts. The team began by pursuing several theories: The cause believed by some team members to be that working the graveyard shift caused higher levels of exhaustion, for example. But in testing that theory against similar comparisons in shifts for other divisions, no rational correlation could be found. Next, the team analyzed whether line foremen were doing their jobs. And then the team analyzed the line procedure itself, and found no flaws. Still, defects were noticeably higher than in other shifts and overall productivity was far lower.

It was not until the team looked deeper that they found the answer. All trainees in the company were assigned to the third shift. The original policy was based on concerns that trainees would slow down the line and efficiency would suffer on all shifts. So trainees dominated the third shift. The team concluded that lower productivity and higher defect rates were normal for the shift because trainees could not be expected to function at *normal* rates for fully trained employees. The decision to place trainees on the same shift made sense, too. Otherwise, the entire processing for other shifts would be slowed down due to the training curve.

This example demonstrates that what is perceived originally as *the problem* is not always the problem at all. In this case, the issue was that the newly acquired subsidiary had instituted a procedure that made sense. The specific attributes for units of production required training of a meticulous nature, so the real problem was not one of productivity. It was lack of complete understanding by the Six Sigma team as to the nature and mix of shifts in the manufacturing environment.

Key Point We cannot enter a project believing that we already know all about the problem. There will be instances where our *lack* of understanding prevents our discovery of a solution.

We cannot apply one set of standards to every problem or project. Just as process and personal problems have to be distinguished and studied differently, we also have to make careful distinctions between *product* and *service* defects. We cannot apply the same engineering standards used in assembly line analysis to the work of the mail room, typing pool, Accounting Department, or other administrative area. The intangible nature of many services presents a special challenge to the Six Sigma team. Identifying defects, monitoring them, and measuring improvements has to all be done based on the nature of the process itself.

Chapter

Product and Service Defects

In some foreign country a priest, a lawyer, and a Six Sigma Black Belt are about to be guillotined. The priest puts his head on the block, they pull the rope, and nothing happens—he declares that he's been saved by divine intervention—so he's let go. The lawyer is put on the block, and again the rope doesn't release the blade. He claims he can't be executed twice for the same crime, and he is set free, too. They grab the Black Belt and shove his head into the guillotine. He looks up at the release mechanism and says, "Wait a minute, I see your problem . . ."

—Reprinted with permission, www.isixsigma.com

Defects—no matter what the cause—can be studied from several different angles, or points of view. But there is always a reason, and once we come to understand the reasons behind the defects, we can eliminate the frequency of those defects—not completely, and not all the time, but enough so that the rate of defects will fall.

Some Six Sigma processes involve the use of technical language, but it really comes down to a fairly straightforward process. In Six Sigma, we:

✔ Define a problem or series of problems, characterized by the defects that have been experienced in the past. (Define)

✔ Identify the causes of the defects. (Measure)

✔ Estimate the cost of defects. (Analyze)

✔ Take steps to fix those defects. (Improve)

✔ Watch the results of our changes. (Control)

The DMAIC process is the core of the Six Sigma working model, and whether you use highly technical language and graphics, or simply make checklists and follow the defects through the system to figure out how to remove them, the end result should be the same. For example, you might say that a particular defect involves "cross functionality" or instead you might observe that a defect involves two or more departments.

For the purpose of understanding the concepts behind the Six Sigma process, we do not use terms that are not needed. The acronyms and abbreviations we employ in this book are widely recognized and used throughout the Six Sigma world; because they are universal, we have used them here as well. In your own company, the use of terms and acronyms will probably vary depending on the point of view of your Six Sigma leadership, the complexity of projects, and the size and scope of the work involved.

Key Point   In Six Sigma projects, simplicity of terminology is preferred; in some cases, more complex terms and tools are justified, but not always.

You will be expected to confront two broad types of defects: tangible or intangible. A "tangible" defect is one that can be easily quantified. For example, on an assembly line, you can count the number of units produced in a shift, and you can identify exactly how many of those units were defective. If your standard is to have 5 percent or fewer defects, but they have been running between 15 percent and 20 percent, you have a problem. Under a Six Sigma project, it would not be adequate to say, "The shift supervisor has to make those employees pay more attention" and then merely assume that will fix the problem. You need to ask many other questions, such as:

✔ Are the raw materials adequate for this product?

✔ Have we changed materials or suppliers lately? Is the raw material different?

✔ Are employees properly trained?

✔ Is our machinery properly set? Can settings be adjusted and if so, does the adjustment level contribute to the defect?

✔ Is the 5 percent standard realistic? If not, what is a realistic standard?

✔ What other possible contributing factors are causing these defects?

In the tangible world, we can locate the causes of defects by asking these questions. The process is itself tangible because we can easily count units of production and spot defects. It is specific. In comparison, an intangible product or service is much harder to measure. Both "units of production" (or, using the Six Sigma phrase, "opportunities") and the number of defects may be far more difficult to count and, as a result, more difficult to correct. This is the challenge for anyone on a Six Sigma team involving intangible services and their defects.

MEASURING VARIANCE

The traditional measurement of defects, often expressed as variance, requires a reliable method for computing the normal expectations. Statisticians use a lot of formulation to arrive at what is called *standard normal* outcome. This is the normal distribution when the mean, or average, outcome is defined as zero, and a standard deviation is 1.

This is one of many ways to calculate and to assign a value to defects. A standard normal outcome would be the overall expectation, based on averages, of what you would be likely to experience in a series of tests. This type of analysis, popular in a manufacturing and production environment where thousands of units are produced, has a valid application. In such an environment, a change of a small degree could mean a big difference in profitability through reduced waste, faster production time, accuracy, and other measurements. Cost accountants are also aware of the big differences that small changes make.

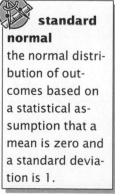

standard normal the normal distribution of outcomes based on a statistical assumption that a mean is zero and a standard deviation is 1.

Key Point Attention to small details often yields big changes. If the nature of a project involves many operations, the more attention to detail, the higher the yield.

Without requiring ourselves to become statisticians, engineers, or cost accountants, we can still devise accurate methods for measuring outcomes and for identifying ways to reduce defects. Six Sigma may have originated as a quality-related theory in a highly technical environment, but it is desirable to make the techniques available to as many nontechnical people as possible.

If you work in a strictly production-related environment, you already know how defects are measured. Units of production and defect-free outcome define a particular shift's work level, or a particular line's *improvement* over previously established levels. Statisticians and accountants are obsessed with *trends* and changes, and they measure the success and effectiveness of change in terms of how those trends evolve. But it is not just the statistician or accountant; in one way or another, everyone is involved with measuring, evaluating, and controlling trends.

For example, if your work is strictly administrative, you have probably identified and defined a form of quality and you understand defects. A Word Processing Department, for example, may use several devices to ensure that the reports, letters, and other documents they process are fully accurate. Statistical reports have to be carefully double-checked to make sure no math errors go through. Spell-checkers can be run against text documents and further edited to find errors in word usage, grammar, and formatting of documents. Many different skills and techniques can be employed to ensure that defects are held to a minimum.

In this environment, a "unit" may be defined as a single document or even as a page within a larger document. A defect could be defined as any error: spelling, word usage, grammar, math errors within the document, formatting inconsistencies, or even a smudge on the edge of the page. The definition of "defect" is going to depend on the precise nature of work that is processed and this example—which is tangible but with a nonspecific unit count—defines the elusiveness of defining defect-free processes.

If we were to apply the strict standards of production, a "unit" would be each and every word within a document. In place of a word, a mathematical value or total would also represent a unit. Such detail, however, makes no sense in a statistical Word Processing Department or secretarial pool. The "unit of production" is probably the document and any defects in the document are important. We would expect to create procedures to locate defects in *draft* form, so that these could be fixed before documents were released to the customer (executive, manager, supervisor, fellow employee, committee, board, etc.). Certainly, you would not want a math error to be found in the middle of an accounting review meeting, or an obvious spelling error to be found by the recipient of a letter from your CEO. Procedures should be designed to ensure that (1) defects can be found in a consistent manner, (2) there is a process in place to correct defects, and (3) continual review is designed and implemented to keep the rate of defects as low as possible. We would be misguided to believe that it would ever be possible to completely eliminate those defects; it is enough to find and correct them before output occurs.

Key Point A discovered *defect* can and should be corrected during the process and in a proactive manner; and not after the output has occurred, in a reactive manner.

Even in a service or administrative department, as long as a process is predictable (meaning, of course, that you know exactly what occurs within that process) and as long as you know the types of defects, or errors, that are likely to occur, then you can determine what controls will be required to reduce defects. In the next chapter, the horizontal work flowchart is set up to demonstrate the types of control points where special care has to be given. For example, when a manager dictates a report and delivers it to a word processing pool, several possible defects can occur. If the report includes grammatical errors, will the word processor be able to catch it? Working from dictation, it is possible to misunderstand and key in the wrong word. Consider a list of words or phrases that could be heard wrong or easily be mistyped:

Correct Word	Heard As	Correct Word	Heard As
a priori	a priority	listened	listed
better	bitter	meant	mint
costing	causing	nullify	notify
dollar	duller	opinion	open
east	eased	preference	reference
familiar	familial	query	clearly
guest	guessed	restitution	resolution

This list points out the need for careful editing. Spell checking is not enough. So here we have an example of potential defects that could easily occur in the weak link between a dictated letter and the processing of the tape. A second defect may occur at the proofreading stage where, instead of looking only for misspelled words, the individual does not also *read* the material to ensure that mistakes do not go through. So the sentence may read "Our client has asked for a summary of items causing this amount of overrun, and is familial with common reasons for such errors." It should be corrected, replacing the word "causing" with "costing" and replacing the word "familial" with "familiar." The first error may be difficult to find in all cases, so in order to entirely eliminate defects, we would depend on both states of the process to work well. It demonstrates, however, that we will not always be able to find the defects themselves. So all a Six Sigma project can do is to identify likely problems and do everything possible to eliminate them.

Are some defects impossible to measure? For example, going back to the word processing pool, what if the need to replace the word "causing" with "costing" is never found? If the word used accidentally conveys approximately the same idea, does this count as a defect of the same level as a word change that completely changes the sentence's meaning? This is a difficult question, because every circumstance (like every example of word replacement) will contain subtle degrees of severity. A word processing employee who makes a lot of mistakes and does not find or correct them presents a training problem, and requires double-checking by other employees as well. So the importance a particular employee attaches to error-free processing is an attribute that is difficult to measure. This makes it even more difficult to identify the likelihood of defects occurring within a department, when every employee may also apply different standards to their own work. What is acceptable? What is not?

One challenge for the Six Sigma team working in an environment with intangible processes, is to define expectations and requirements of the customer. So in a word processing pool, for example, the expectation might be for error-free documents, and the requirement may be that all documents are double-checked prior to release. This may be the case for statistical reporting more than for text documents. For example, if the Accounting Department presents budgets, financial statements, and cost estimates to be prepared, these should be checked by at least two people in the department preparing the work, and a draft checked again by someone in the Accounting Department—all before final release.

The conflict often arises between the time needed to thoroughly execute work and deadlines. If a math-intensive document of many pages is presented for fast processing, and has to be completed within a few hours, that means (1) employees will feel pressured to work faster, meaning that (2) more errors are going to be made, and (3) less time will be available to double-check. So one *defect* in this process is the time pressure involved in how and when work has to be done. So a second challenge to the Six Sigma team in dealing with such defects is to identify the causes beyond actual processing. In this example, input was late enough so that output was required within an unreasonable amount of time. As a result, either the work cannot be delivered as demanded, or it will be on time but probably with a greater frequency of errors. For a financial report, any errors are going to be unacceptable. The individual reviewing a financial report will have both an expectation and a requirement that the report be accurate. So it would be preferable for the report to be delivered late, than it would be to make a quick deadline but issue the report with many errors.

This example demonstrates that pinning down a definition of a defect is not always going to be limited to the specific error that becomes obvious right away. A defect may be found in an unreasonable deadline; in poor quality of information or raw material provided (a difficult to hear transcription, for example); or in the attitude of the poorly-trained employee. A lot of variances come into the picture, and a Six Sigma team should be able to consider the full range of possible problems in its analytical approach to identifying and solving problems.

VARIANCE AND IMPROVEMENT TESTING

Anyone who has never been involved with the actual testing of variances, knows that those variances themselves can be elusive, multifaceted, and ever-changing. It is rare to discover a variance that is (1) easily identified, (2) stationary, and (3) easily remedied. If variances did contain these attributes, they would be *easy* to fix. We have to assume, as a starting point in the study of variances, that the easy ones are eliminated in due course, and that the Six Sigma team is assigned to tackle the particularly tough variances that remain chronically unchanged.

Key Point If finding and eliminating defects is easy, then those changes occur during the process. Six Sigma teamwork is needed when the problems are more complex and when they involve many people and departments.

Applying the scientific method to variance testing, we would have to begin with a basic hypothesis: *What is the definition of the* problem *we are supposed to address?* In the example previously mentioned of the late deliveries coming from Shipping and Receiving, the initial belief is that the shipping employees are not doing their jobs. In a methodical analysis of the problem, we discover that it is far more widespread and complex, and will require changes in many departments: Sales, Marketing, Accounting, Inventory Control, and Shipping and Receiving. So in defining the problem, we discover the true scope and realize that it is not a simple one to fix. We cannot simply call the manager and say, "Send stuff out on time," because the issues involve other process problems, and all of those have to be fixed before we can expect Shipping and Receiving to do their job.

The next step in the testing process is, again, another question: *What are we supposed to test?* There are many elements to consider, referring to the SIPOC process map: Suppliers, Input, Process, Output, and Customers. Any or all of these segments may involve areas requiring testing, and as part of the definition of what to test, each of these areas should be examined to find potential problems. Returning to the example of Shipping and Receiving, a number of potential problem areas come up at each of these segments. For example:

Suppliers: Are materials being provided on time? If not, why not? How can this problem be corrected effectively and immediately? What internal processes have to change to facilitate timely delivery? ("Suppliers" may be defined as outside vendors for delivery of shipping supplies or the sales reps who need to deliver orders for action, so even this phase is complex in the definition itself.)

Input: Is the Marketing Department processing orders in a timely manner? In fact, why do they have to be involved in processing between sales reps and Shipping/Receiving? How can the process be improved for faster delivery of orders?

Process: What inventory problems make it difficult to fill orders? What is the cause of those problems? How can back order volume be reduced? How can inventory controls be improved? Do we even know what is in inventory right now? What changes have to be made in this system?

Output: What elements prevent prompt shipment in each point along the process? Since output involves several increments, where do we need to make changes?

What specific problems in Shipping and Receiving have to be changed? What changes have to be made in the Accounting Department to ensure that basic shipping supplies are on hand when needed?

Customers: What expectations are not being met? What requirements are not being met? Is three-day delivery a realistic goal? Do customers expect this? Would customers be just as happy with a seven-day promise of shipment, for example? Are we doing harm to ourselves by having sales reps make unrealistic commitments? If the three-day shipping promise *is* realistic, what list of changes are needed to ensure that we meet it all the time?

The third step in variance testing using the scientific method, is *How will our proposed changes affect revenues and earnings?* The cost element is an integral part of any customer service project. And given the Six Sigma philosophy, *all* projects are related to customer service in some form or another. We need to perform an analysis of how projects increase revenues or reduce costs and expenses, so that earnings are improved. From the corporate and financial point of view, this is going to be the ultimate center of judgment. Appropriately so, the CEO and CFO of the organization and all managers in the reporting chain have questions on their minds at all times: How does a particular decision affect profits? Why is this appropriate? If the company is in the business of earning profits for its shareholders, it is a responsibility of management to pursue ever-growing revenue volume and profits, ensuring that costs and expenses are held to a reasonable level and otherwise promoting the shareholders' interests. With this in mind, it is everyone's job within the company to become part of the "profit team" and to recognize this agenda as part of everyone's job.

Today, many people view corporate profits as distasteful or shameful but, in fact, it is the generation point of jobs. Beyond the pure profit motive, companies have a responsibility for the welfare of their employees, another aspect in the well-designed Six Sigma program. If we integrate the philosophies of "profit motive" and "employee relations" into a single point of view, then we have a powerful and potentially revolutionary change for the better in how we approach the whole question of customer service. As GE's well-known CEO expressed this integrated approach, "One thing we have discovered with certainty is that anything we do that makes the customer more successful inevitably results in a financial return for us."[1]

Key Point There really is not a conflict between good service and the profit motive. They are different aspects of the same corporate culture, and reflect the desire to excel.

The fourth step in variance testing is: *How do we expect our changes to affect customer response, and how are we better meeting customer expectations and requirements?* Without this critical analysis of what are, in effect, *goals* to the Six Sigma project, we have no way to understand whether our work is effective. By identifying our expectations in terms of improved customer expectations and requirements, we are able to add a quantifiable element to even the most intangible of service projects. We can produce a means for monitoring success, a budget of the project's results, and then compare those outcome budgets to actual responses.

Finally, we address the question: *How do our changes effectively reduce future defects?* The internal controls that are developed as an essential element of the project, ultimately determine how effectively our variance analysis worked. In a successful outcome, future defects are reduced permanently, because the changes in processes find and correct emerging variances before the output gets into the customer's hands. We cannot eliminate defects entirely, but we can create system processes (or internal controls) that check and re-check for variances and find them. In a sense, we can describe this concept as "correcting emerging input or process variances before they turn into process or output defects." While achieving Six Sigma output—3.4 variances per million opportunities—is obviously not possible, we can eliminate an incredible number of variances under this definition, primarily by creating strong, reliable, and consistent internal controls, check points, and elimination of root causes of those variances.

CRITICAL TO QUALITY (CTQ) MEASUREMENTS

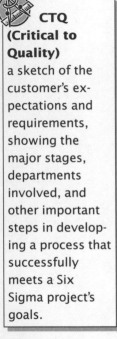

CTQ (Critical to Quality) a sketch of the customer's expectations and requirements, showing the major stages, departments involved, and other important steps in developing a process that successfully meets a Six Sigma project's goals.

Lean Six Sigma (LSS) a system combining the concepts of Six Sigma with those of lean manufacturing, a system designed to improve cyclical efficiency and reduce or eliminate waste in processes.

In preparation for the detailed horizontal flowchart we review in Chapter 6, it will be necessary to sketch out our preliminary priorities list. We may call this list any number of things, but its purpose is to identify the elements of the process that are essential: the customer's major requirements and expectations, the process requirements necessary to support the customer, and any specific details that go into that process. We may think of this as a "rough draft" of the detailed flowchart we will prepare in the next chapter.

In Six Sigma lingo, this rough draft is called the *CTQ (Critical to Quality)* tree. It is a sketch, preferably moving left to right (rather than top to bottom) showing a customer's anticipated experience as he or she moves through our process. It is especially useful to prepare a CTQ tree when multiple departments are involved.

The CTQ tree is a graphic expression of a customer's expectations and requirements. Under the concepts of *Lean Six Sigma (LSS)*, the CTQ tree is considered an essential element in identifying the customer and his or her needs; and the customer is all important. One expert has stated that "The customer is king in LSS. If it weren't for customers, an organization would not exist. Therefore, people need to link all improvement activities, metrics, and investments to the customer."[2]

An example of a CTQ tree is shown in Figure 5.1.

In this example—which can also serve as a preliminary rough draft for the more detailed horizontal worksheet in the next chapter—we have attempted to zero in on the *major* process areas requiring attention of the Six Sigma team. The purpose here is to highlight areas needing the most attention, the most critical process points, or the points where we would expect to see the most severe weak links in the process.

Key Point   Like all other artists, the Six Sigma team starts with its rough sketch—the CTQ tree—and from

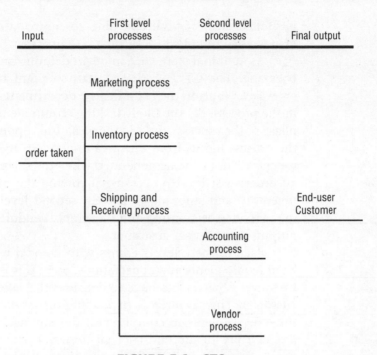

FIGURE 5.1 CTQ tree.

there builds its masterpiece, the elegant solution to a well-defined problem.

We do not attempt in the CTQ tree to construct a complete flowchart with interactive loops or checkpoints for defects. The purpose is to provide the Six Sigma team with a broad overview and outline of the areas needing attention. So a team member who is not immediately familiar with the entire range of problems (likely to be *most* team members) will have a good jump on what needs to be done within the defined project. Most team members will have a point of view about a segment of the problem, but few if any will initially understand the full scope. For example, a Six Sigma team for this problem could consist of one employee each from Sales, Marketing, Inventory, Shipping and Receiving, and Accounting departments. None of these people will necessarily appreciate the range of problems that the sponsor (perhaps a Marketing vice president for this particular project) will be able to appreciate—which brings us to the purpose of the CTQ process.

As an initial step, we can begin defining areas worth checking. The CTQ is a good starting point because it shows everyone on the team (1) the departments involved in the process, (2) the likely tasking requirements in each phase of the process, and (3) the weak links, points where the process moves from one area to another. In this case, we show "input" being generated when the sales rep takes an order; first level processing involving the marketing, inventory, and shipping processes; second level processing involving accounting and the supply vendor; and final output, the end-user customer.

Each of these levels comes with its own process-related requirements and expectations. So in this regard, the first level departments have to consider the sales rep as a customer. The sales rep is depending on service from all three departments to comply with the promise for three-day delivery to the end-user customer. The Accounting Department (second level) should treat all first level departments as its customer in addition to the obvious customer relationship it has with the outside vendor. Finally, the end-user customer probably is aware of a customer relationship with the sales rep who, in the customer's mind, *is* "the company" with all of its internal processes. The sales rep is the individual making the promise that "your purchase will be shipping within three days." The customer does not care what is involved internally; the only issue is whether or not that promise is kept. But while the customer is not concerned with *how* the promise is kept, the Six Sigma team certainly is concerned. The CTQ is the starting point for identifying the players, their needs, and their processes; the defects that grow from the process itself; and the changes needed to fix that process.

THE INTERNAL DEFECT ISSUE—IS IT IMPORTANT?

So many customer service programs emphasize end-user customers, to a fault. If a department is concerned *only* with the first and last elements of a process—from input to output—without regard for what goes on in between, how can a process be improved? If the solution to a perceived customer service problem is to set up a department to respond to customer complaints, this creates more problems than it solves:

✔ *It is a reactive approach.* The reactive approach is appropriate for some kinds of problems, notably those that we cannot anticipate. But customer complaints are highly predictable. An analysis of the process from input through output will point quite specifically to areas where the internal process can and will fail. By removing those failure points, or invitations to defects, we immediately improve overall efficiency, cost, and end-user satisfaction. The Customer Service department that is set up to give some form of remuneration to an unhappy customer is often more irritating than helpful. For example, if you were unhappy with your room in a hotel, does it address the problem to be presented with a coupon for a free room in the future? If you did not enjoy your meal at a restaurant, will a discount make the problem go away? Reactive customer service treats symptoms, often impotently, without attacking the real causes of defects.

Key Point The reactive approach—what used to be called Management by Exception—works in some situations, but *not* in service. By the time you have to react, the damage has already been done.

✔ *By design, it cannot address the underlying problems.* The customer service department that operates in isolation from the internal process is specifically designed to *not* solve the real problem. If management believes this is a cheap solution to complaints, they are quite mistaken. It is expensive because it does not find and fix the problems causing those complaints. If the *problem* is that shipments are breaking during shipping, the *solution* is to improve packaging design, not to send another order out. If the *problem* is that delivery promises are not being kept, the *solution* is not to demand faster work from your Shipping Department if, in fact, the root problems reside elsewhere.

✔ *In all likelihood, problems are going to recur and defects will not be fixed.* There is no real value in the creation of a customer response team if the problems remain and are likely to recur. So many managers believe that prompt response, courteous treatment, and the combined investigation and fix, are all that is required, and that this tactic will create an impression in the market that your company is responsive. It would be far better if the market perceived the company as so dependable and high-quality in its customer service that there is rarely any problem to which the company needs to react. Let us face it: Once a customer has to call in with a complaint, the system has already failed. While that customer's failed expectations have to be fixed as quickly as possible, it is equally important to trace the process back through to the point of failure, and to then take action to prevent it from recurring. This is where most customer service systems fail.

✔ *You cannot understand the causes of customer complaints if you don't examine how they came about.* The entire premise of customer service is going to be based on one of two broad assumptions. The traditional assumption is that the process "is what it is" and there is going to be a level of defects. Customers complain; we fix. The second premise is that we do not want customer complaints, because we need to design our processes so that variances never reach the point of turning into defects. The Six Sigma approach is to make a distinction between a variance and a defect. A variance is an emerging defect that, if caught in time, can be adjusted in the internal process loop, so that the defect is caught and prevented in time.

Now given these observations about customer service shortcomings, how do we apply these principles to our *internal* customer, the other departments and people we deal with every day? Perhaps a more appropriate question is: Do we give the internal customer the same level of importance and the same priority as we give to the end-user, external customer?

Is the idea of the internal customer just a quality program theme, a way to try to get people to think in terms of service excellence? Or in fact, does the application of this idea mean a radical change in the way internal departments and people deal with one another? The experiences of Motorola, GE, and other companies that pioneered the Six Sigma idea and molded it into an effective tool for changing the corporate culture, will insist that the Six Sigma approach works—because it puts concepts into action and helps everyone within the company to see customers everywhere they look. They may not use the precise terminology of "internal customer" to describe the change in attitude, but it is a change by whatever name we call these relationships.

Key Point One thing we can learn from the team approach to Six Sigma: Everyone is in the customer service business.

If we are to permanently improve the way we relate to the end-user customer or client, we need to take the improved attitude all the way through our internal processes, and overlap a service mentality on each and every point in that process where one person or department deals with another. Whether delivering or receiving information, products, reports, statements, requests, or other forms of input and output, the whole process counts as service.

Once we begin to recognize the universal aspects of the service mentality, the whole idea of Six Sigma makes sense. It becomes obvious that the big question, Are internal customers important? is the same question as, Are customers important? We can only serve our customers by removing those defects and by preventing their recurrence by improving processes. That may require continual monitoring, change, improvement, modification, and ultimately, revamping entire processes as growth occurs. Today's working system may be obsolete tomorrow; in fact, the nature of growth itself requires constant change in internal systems. The translation of this may well be "Customer service is a constantly changing aspect of the corporate culture." Even if your work involves little human contact, that customer is out there. If you did not have customers, you would not have a job.

REEXAMINING INITIAL ASSUMPTIONS—ARE YOU CORRECT?

A final step in the analytical process of defining where variances and defects are likely to occur is to once again question your initial assumptions. In so many quality projects, a team begins under the assumptions that a particular problem has to be fixed, only to discover that in fact the problem originally defined to create the project is not the problem at all. For example, let us say that your Six Sigma team is given the project to "Find out why so many check requests arrive in the Accounting Department outside of normal match cycles." In other words, the team's job is to figure out how to get sales reps, other departments, and individuals to understand the accounting cycle and to time check requests accordingly. However, upon examination of the realities of the process, your team discovers that this is *not* a problem of people needing to comply with twice-monthly batch cycles; the real problem is that the Accounting Department does not run cycles often enough. We have previously mentioned the idea of having two major cycles per month timed for the second and fourth weeks, and then adding two minor cycles to occur in between. In this simplified example, the initial problem of noncompliance by everyone in the company, is replaced (and, in fact, solved) by the practical idea of changing the cyclical limitations employed by the Accounting Department. This type of evolution in problem solving (including the change from initial assumption to a more expanded realm of problems) is typical of the kind of process you can expect in a Six Sigma project environment. It allows individuals to look at problems creatively, to bring different aspects of the problem to bear in designing solutions, and, of course, to constantly question underlying assumptions.

Key Point Rushing to find the *answers* is premature, especially if you do not yet understand the right *questions* that you should be asking.

The "assumption"—that thing or series of things that we believe are the problem or the cause of the problem—is a difficult matter to contend with. So many so-called quality programs are designed with a solution-focused mentality, without giving consideration to the possibility that the problem itself is *not* the right issue to address. This is especially true when a sacred cow is in the way of a solution. For example, if the unofficial word is that whatever solutions a team arrives at, the top executives are to be treated as *exceptions*—meaning you cannot impose rules to change their behavior—then the original assumptions of the quality effort are flawed. The assumption should be that a problem exists and has to be fixed, and that the recommendations provided by a Six Sigma team apply to everyone. Otherwise, why waste our time?

A related problem arises when someone, often a manager, is so committed to an original assumption that he or she cannot let go of it, even when the Six Sigma team produces proof that the problem is something else, more complex, or that the original assumption itself is *wrong*.

These problems are dispensed with when the Six Sigma approach is based on the scientific method. As long as the leadership council and sponsor accept the premise that analysis is going to begin and then proceed on a fact-finding basis, the project will have a far better chance of success. The scientific method is free of political, power, or other self-interested motives. It is designed to examine the facts and to draw conclusions without any underlying assumptions getting in the way. The reason that assumptions cause so many problems is that they are usually developed with lack of a factual base. For example, we see assumptions all the time in the corporate world, and before we can improve links between operating units, departments, and individuals, we have to get rid of those assumptions. For example:

> *Marketing Department assumption:* "Those accountants have no idea what it's like out here because they never see a customer. To them, it's all about the numbers."
>
> *Accounting Department assumption:* "Sales reps couldn't document their way out of a wet paper bag. Their focus is shallow; all they want is to get paid right now, no matter what point we're at in the cycle."
>
> *Shipping and Receiving Department assumption:* "Everyone thinks we have it so easy, and they yell at us when things go out late—even though they bring everything down here at ten to five on Friday afternoon."
>
> *Word Processing Pool assumption:* "No one understands that it takes time to input a lengthy document. This 'hurry up and wait' attitude is what causes errors."

All of these observations, assumptions, and beliefs—and others just like them—are outgrowths of poor internal communication. The Six Sigma project is designed not only to solve the real, well-defined, and thoroughly-researched *problem*. It also provides people from different departments to take part in a broader-view effort to fix problems. It lets people recognize how problems really develop, to see that they usually involve the participation and contribution of many departments, and rarely just one. The less complex problems are easily fixed and probably never make it to the Six Sigma project team level. This is where everyone in the company has the chance to expand their "corporate view"—the company-specific version of the world view. Since the corporation is the world for many employees, this exposure to many different points of view of the same problem (often like the parable of the blind men and the elephant) is enlightening.[3] All are correct insofar as their experience and exposure allow; but all points of view are also incomplete. Involvement in Six Sigma allows each individual to see the whole problem and, thus, qualifies them to better work together to arrive at effective and permanent solutions.

Key Point The typical problems a Six Sigma team is asked to tackle *are* a lot like an elephant being described by blind men. We need all of their observations in order to understand what the problem looks like.

This is essential because, in order to arrive at a valid answer, we need to ensure that our assumptions are correct to begin with. This is an important concept in market testing and in statistics, as it is in project analysis. For example, a testing company wants to test market a new product. So it sets up a sample stand in a local super market between 5:30 and 6:30 P.M. for three weekdays in a row. Based on promising responses from a majority of shoppers, the product is mass produced and placed in stores all around the country. But sales are very poor and the company loses millions. Why? Upon reevaluation of the initial assumptions, the company finally realizes its error. By limiting its test hour to the 5:30 to 6:30 P.M. hour, most shoppers were not the family's *primary* shopper. The majority of people in the stores at that hour are buying items on the way home from work. The *primary* shopper is more likely to arrive at the store in the early afternoon, a time period that was not tested.

In this example, the market test was performed on the wrong audience. So an initial assumption, when determined to be in error, can cost millions in product investment and lost revenue. If we take this example and apply it to a variety of projects, we can easily see how initial assumptions are easily misdirected because information is incomplete, or because the assumed problem is only a symptom of a much larger problem. So if the Marketing vice president begins to analyze late delivery problems with the assumption that "Those guys in Shipping are messing up our marketing plan," and a project proceeds on that basis, the real problem is not going to be solved. The project defined as How do we make Shipping more efficient? will evolve into a more comprehensive expression: How can we improve processes in Sales, Marketing, Inventory Control, Accounting, and Shipping so that end-user shipments can be made in a timely manner? This is an entirely different project because the initial assumption has changed.

The next chapter moves these ideas and observations to the next step: developing the work flow on the horizontal diagram to (1) identify the key elements on the SIPOC process map, (2) analyze likely weak links where variances are likely to occur, (3) develop ways to catch variances in order to prevent them from becoming defects, and (4) monitor the improved process to permanently eliminate the most common occurrences of defects.

Chapter

Improving Process Systems

Watching the old I Love Lucy shows as a child, I remember a conversation with my mother. In the famous scene in the chocolate packing plant, the conveyor belt is moving too quickly and Lucy begins stuffing chocolates into her mouth. I asked my mother, "Why don't they slow down that belt?" My mother replied, "Sometimes, these things just happen. Just watch the show."

Of course, these things do "just happen." But in spite of the set-up for the sake of the comedy, I still find myself wondering Why don't they slow down that belt?

Once a Six Sigma team is formed and given a project to perform, several elements of the project have to be defined, in addition to the exact problem. These elements include a budget (if applicable), schedule, and deadlines. If the problem is that a production belt moves too quickly, then it would not make sense to analyze worker exhaustion, manufacturing standards, or packaging. The problem is that the belt is going too quickly. In the complexities of the workplace, not every problem is so easy to spot; that's why we need processes to define problems, hopefully before we begin solving them.

The budget is set to specify what costs and expenses will be incurred in completing the project tasks. For example, it might be necessary to hire an outside consultant, pay for research materials, and assign employee time to the team's work. (If the corporate policy is to set up an employee labor budget as a separate operating function outside the employee's department, this can be a major segment of the budget. The Accounting Department would assign a portion of each team member's salary and benefits, to the team's effort to come to a reasonable cost total. In this way, management can measure the cost of Six Sigma projects, versus estimated cost reduction benefits.)

The schedule has to be based on a realistic estimate of how much time will be needed to complete the project. Considering that team members need to continue performing the functions of their fulltime jobs, scheduling for team projects may be particularly difficult, politically sensitive, and subject to change. If and when other priorities arise, it may be necessary to either delay meetings or work around a department's schedule. So the Six Sigma project schedule has to be quite flexible. It should have built-in flexibility so that the team can work around each team member's conflicts without causing excessive delays.

At the conclusion of the schedule is a deadline. Successful projects should include progress deadlines as well as a final deadline. Each deadline should define what the team hopes to achieve by a particular point. Without a deadline, there is no incentive to push forward and complete the tasks assigned to the team. If we think of the deadline as a "time budget," it helps to understand the importance of setting time limits, both for segments of the project and for final completion. Some segments may be overlapping, so when different team members are assigned specific tasks, it does not always mean that the work of other members has to stop completely.

Key Point Building deadlines into the process analysis helps to budget time effectively, and to test the efficiency of current processes.

One of the primary tasks for the team is to identify work flow in the process. This is essential for identifying where and when variances are likely to occur; how those variances can be managed before defects occur; and what other actions are needed. For example, some processes fall apart because input is inaccurate, and others fail because processes are delayed. In either case, these variances are predictable. There are points in every process where they are likely to occur, and the key to improving processes is to review all steps and then make changes to ensure a better overall process—meaning managed variances, reduced defects, identified weak links, and new elements to the process. In this chapter, we develop a detailed horizontal to document procedures involving delivery of customer orders. We first develop a worksheet showing how the process works currently, and then make specific recommendations to remove variances and improve the overall process.

FORMS OF VISUAL PROCESS PLANNING

Some Six Sigma processes depend heavily on a variety of charting tools. While some of these are essential, particularly in technical and complex projects, the actual level of charting you use in your project should be dictated by the requirements of the assignment. You should avoid dependence on charts in place of practical solutions. Charting is a valuable tool in identifying problems, analyzing trends, and figuring out where to fix what is not working. Your efforts should be geared toward development of the work flow process chart, which can also be called the *horizontal flowchart*. This tool is designed to methodically identify all the important elements of processes: who performs the work, a timeline, documentation that flows from the process, points where work process moves from one person or department to another (the weak links of the process), and loops in the process (decision points as well as points where variances appear and can be looped back to previous steps for correction).

    The tools that you can encounter in your own internal

horizontal flowchart a tool used to visually document the way that processes work; and to identify points where variances are likely to occur. The purpose of the flowchart is to help the Six Sigma team develop improved systems and suggest changes to reduce defects.

Six Sigma process may include any number of charts. All should be used primarily as tools to help develop the horizontal flowchart. These other charts may include:

✔ CPM (Critical Path Method)—a chart involving identified steps connected with lines to help visualize steps in the process.

✔ PERT (Program Evaluation and Review Technique)—a charting system used to identify minimum and maximum time requirements.

✔ Vertical flowcharts—traditional top-to-bottom procedural summaries, a format more comfortable for many people than the horizontal method (and useful for serving as a transitional work process descriptive tool).

✔ Organizational charts—a tool used to explain a hierarchy within a company or department, useful for explaining how and why processes flow the way they do.

✔ Frequency distribution charts—usually consisting of a series of x's in a distribution field, a visual tool showing the number of times events occur over a period of time.

✔ Pie charts—circular visual aids showing how parts of a whole are distributed, often used in presentations. For example, Where a Dollar of Revenue Goes would be a chart showing how money is spent. For project purposes, a pie chart can be helpful in selling ideas to decision makers.

✔ Checklists—primarily narrative tools listing singular or comparative elements, useful for decision making and for brainstorming work.

✔ CTQ trees (see Chapter 5)—a visual representation of work flow, used for overview before more detailed flowcharting begins.

✔ Tradition-based coded flowcharts—whether vertical or horizontal, this flowchart uses particular shapes to denote actions or events. These often are called "activity flow" summaries. An oval indicates the start or stop points. Decisions are shown as diagonal squares. Steps are rectangular. Arrow boxes may be used to show direction. These varying shapes are useful in flowcharts because they help us to distinguish among different types of operations, especially in very complex processes. For example, if we wish to find the decision points, we can simply seek out the particular shape used for that operation, and then review what occurs before, during, and after the decision itself. This is a convenient way to zero in on potential problem areas within the work flow. The typical uses of shapes are summarized in Figure 6.1.

✔ Line graphs—a square or rectangular box with one or more lines moving across from left to right.

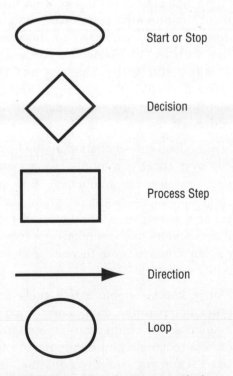

Figure 6.1 Flowcharting symbols.

A common example is a stock price chart, which may show prices as well as a moving average.

✔ Bar charts—a rectangle with fixed value "bins" shown for set values, often over time or in comparison to one another (such as revenues by division for a quarter, for example). A bar chart can be presented with the "bin" values shown horizontally (left to right) or vertically (top to bottom). Some applications of bar charts are also called "histograms."

✔ Pareto charts—combined line and bar charts. Typically, the bar portion would show relative value levels or trends, and the line portion would demonstrate moving averages or accent differences between the bar portions.

✔ Cause and effect flowcharts—horizontal representations of elements affecting a process (shown above or below a central process line. Each element (commonly equipment, employees, vendors, etc.) are connected to the central process line with a grid listing the effects each creates. This is useful in the same way as CTQ trees, because it enables the Six Sigma team to visually identify all the process elements that need to be addressed.

✔ Scatter diagram—a chart showing how events occur over time, commonly using symbols to denote events or frequency. For example, a singular-symbol scatter diagram may consist of small squares; or a multievent depiction might use x's and o's to show relative events. (For example, an x may denote increase and an o may denote decrease.)

✔ Matrix charts—demonstrate cause-and-effect or other comparative data. The format consists of many possible configurations; a popular one is to draw a rectangle and divide in into four equally sized segments. The divisions may be identified as moving from easy to hard or from low to high time requirement; expensive to cheap; high priority to low; and other binary distinctions. The purpose of the matrix form is to identify how occurrences fall within a process, and what types of variances should be expected to occur. The matrix format is also called an "affinity diagram."

✔ Narrative/flowchart combinations—an effective tool for documenting new procedures. More is presented on tools like these in Chapter 7.

✔ Data collection forms—come in a variety of designs, but their purpose is the same: to gather essential information relating to processes, budgets, time constraints, and other important elements the Six Sigma team has to consider in its work.

✔ Outline format lists—a popular method for organizing data is the use of the outline form, in which primary steps can be broken down into any number of sub-groupings. This is a useful tool in gathering information on how processes work.

Visual tools are popular in organizations because they convey information more effectively than pure narrative or lists of numbers. In the computerized world, data can also be organized and quickly converted into chart form. Excel and Word programs include charting functions that enable you to present charts in any number of formats, including 3-D if desired.

Key Point Graphics are powerful tools for communicating ideas and identifying how things are done. However, the graphic tools used in a project should reflect requirements above all else.

Overuse of graphics is tempting, partly because it is so easy and partly because it is one way to present information without having to do a lot of basic research. The flaw is that graphics are not a replacement for hard, reliable facts. Graphics are excellent educational tools and presentation tools (for example, the use of PowerPoint in presentations and meetings), but underlying those graphics, you also need to develop the solid work to back up what those pictures reveal. The graphic is not the product; it is only one of many tools for training, conveying information, and demonstrating trends.

ELEMENTS OF THE FLOWCHART

The horizontal flowchart is the ideal vehicle for (1) identifying even the most complex processes as they are performed today, (2) locating likely weak links (decision points, transfer of process from one person or department to another), and (3) probable solutions. If we view *process variances* as the starting point of defects—a nontraditional definition, but appropriate for our purposes—then we also isolate the methods for removing those variances. A "variance" has a specific definition in statistics, so we will use the term "process variance" to define what we are talking about in the process flowchart. This is the core element of Six Sigma: finding those emerging process variances and creating self-audit loops to stop the variances and to prevent them from producing process and output defects.

The second key to finding and correcting variances is to develop an understanding of who has actual responsibility for processes. We cannot really understand a process by merely listing the steps involved. We have to assign a responsibility for each and every step in that process, so that we can develop a sense of who has the ability to find and correct variances.

Some processes (or segments of larger processes) occur within a single department. Even then, we cannot merely say that the department executes steps in the process. One individual in the department or one area or title is responsible for each step. Other processes are complicated because the work is performed by two or more people or teams, sometimes in different departments. For example, a committee, board, or other team may be assigned the responsibility for a process. While the members will assign functions to sub-teams or individuals, we

 process variances the points within processes where variances emerge; such variances lead to process and output defects unless the process is altered to correct variances along the way.

still need—in our process flowchart—to identify the responsible group. To avoid the confusion of using departments, job titles, or individuals in our descriptions, we instead use the term *area of responsibility* to describe responsibility for process steps. This may be an individual, a department, board, committee, team, or even a subcontractor, separate division, or consultant. The area of responsibility, in whatever configuration, executes the step in the process, and also is able to find and correct variances before the process moves forward.

> **area of responsibility** the person, department, team, board, committee, subcontractor, consultant, or other individual or group, identified as having primary charge over one or more steps in a process.

Is this an important distinction? Why can we not simply come up with some descriptive term without spending a lot of time with such fine-tuning of definitions? The answer also identifies the method for permanently increasing the Sigma and approaching Six Sigma in our process improvements: *The area of responsibility is able to spot variances and to loop the process to eliminate those variances before the process moves forward. No one else can perform this function.*

We cannot assign someone outside the area of responsibility with the task of variance oversight. It simply is not practical. Anyone who works on a process knows that much of the work proceeds in a relatively isolated manner. Each employee processes work alone most of the time, even when the effort is coordinated among many other people. So the area of responsibility (whether a person or a group of people) has to take on the task of checking their own work to find variances. Also within processes, we want to build internal controls enabling each process step to verify the accuracy of the previous step to the degree possible, as a further test of variances.

Key Point Including a timeline with the flowchart helps us grasp the delays that are likely to occur, and how those can be reduced.

Also with the format of the horizontal flowchart is a time line. This provides us with a view of not only what steps are involved (process steps) and who does them (area of responsibility), but also how long it all is supposed to take. So the time line is placed along the area below process steps, with identified dates or times involved in the process.

The overall configuration of the horizontal flowchart shows us all the elements of the process, including the weak links. Any place in the flowchart where the line of process moves from one area of responsibility to another, you have a weak link. Errors occur whenever one area of responsibility passes information, documents, or requests to someone else. This is where we will find the majority of errors, delays, and outright defects. Even when a variance has become a defect, it is still not too late to find it and make corrections. Ultimately, a process defect is not going to affect the outcome as long as it is caught in time. Our Sigma rating is going to be based on output, so catching problems during the process is a valuable internal control mechanism.

As processes are completed, various documents are produced and used by subsequent areas of responsibility. As processes and time lines move left to right, we also highlight the document production step by connecting the process step to an identified document, shown below the process steps and time line. Examples of this are shown later in this chapter.

The horizontal flowchart is an excellent tool for documenting multiphased processes. As everyone in business knows, some processes move from one step to another and are easy to follow; but *most* processes involve multiple areas of responsibility and many *concurrent operations*. The horizontal flowchart enables us to track as many of these concurrent operations as possible. We can follow several areas of responsibility, each moving along its separate process sequence and time line and—when applicable—interacting with other areas of responsibility along the way. Some processes involve concurrent operations along with interaction between two or more of these areas. To fully document how this works, we have to be prepared to use the horizontal flowchart to follow all the process links from beginning to end.

Yet another reality we have to be prepared for in documenting processes is the multiple SIPOC level. In the purely theoretical application of Six Sigma, we can com-

concurrent operations
in a complex process, the involvement of two or more separate areas of responsibility, each performing a series of process steps. Concurrent operations may require linking back and forth between different areas of responsibility, or they may proceed separately until a point where the separate effort is united into a single, concluding series of steps.

prehend SIPOC as a single series of steps, leading from suppliers all the way through to end-user customers. In practice, though, processes tend to involve tiers and levels of SIPOC. In reviewing the phases of a process, we realize that few of our processes are singular. So the horizontal flowchart is valuable in identifying the process steps. SIPOC—as a theory and defining tool—is useful in our initial Six Sigma project phase. However, when it comes to explaining who does what, why, and where the process flows, we discover that the actual work flow is far more complicated. Few things are done with singular SIPOC elements, and few processes move from beginning to end in singular lines.

Even with all of these complexities, we can manage any process, no matter how complex, by using the horizontal flowchart and by following each process from origination to execution. We can also identify likely variance points by the use of various types of loops. The loop is a familiar device in flowcharting from top to bottom. For example, in processing a number of records, the loop is used to identify steps that have to be repeated, and once the loop has been completed, the process moves to the next step. There are three specific types of loops that can be used within a process: (1) decision, (2) repetition, and (3) verification. These are shown in Figure 6.2. We have used the circle as the box to identify the loop. In the decision loop, we have superimposed the decision box over the loop box, indicating that this step involves both operations. This is a key highlight; it implies the high possibility that a variance can occur at this phase.

In the *decision* loop, we determine a binary outcome—yes or no. If the answer to the decision is no, the process loops back to the previous step. This is a typical verify-and-proceed checking process. In the *repetition* loop, a series of steps are repeated until the whole task is done, at which point the process proceeds to the next step. And in the *verification* loop, we are most likely to discover and fix variances. If data is correct, we proceed; if incorrect, we go back to the previous step. This type of loop can and should be inserted anywhere in the process where verification is required. The decision and verification steps are different. A *decision* refers not to incorrect data, but to the possibility that some elements

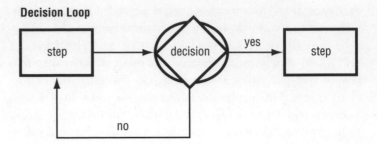

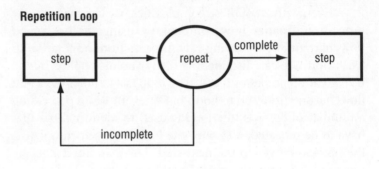

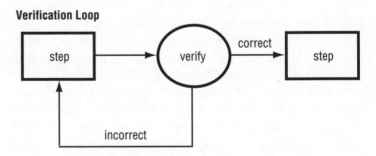

FIGURE 6.2 Types of loop operations.

are incomplete, missing, or uncertain. The decision to proceed is based on whether the process has to continue. For example, some processes would end if the decision went one way, or proceed if it went the other. Such processes may be abbreviated, or extended. For example, in a procedure to check inventory levels, the decision question is: Are there at least 400 units in stock? If the answer is yes, the process ends. If it is no, the process goes forward to another step, ordering more units. (In our illustration, the decision is a loop, which would be applicable when the decision requires *repetition*, returning to the previous step to fill in missing data, for example. In the case of inventory, the decision is whether to continue to another series of steps, or to end the process.)

Key Point The decision loop is the most common, showing where a process moves in one of two directions.

In comparison to the decision, *verification* refers to internal checking, seeking out of possible variances and, if found, returning to the previous step to make corrections. If the verification loop is used in the critical steps of the process, you will be able to prevent variances (thus stopping their outgrowth, defects) within the process. This has a dramatic effect on overall Sigma, with defects falling dramatically.

Key Point The verification loop is a visual representation of how variances are found and fixed before the process goes forward. This is a very important internal control point in every process.

A final note concerning the horizontal flowchart before going to a detailed example: This flowchart is a powerful training tool for new processes or for revised processes. In addition to the detailed flowchart itself, we can break out specific process steps and combine these with step-by-step narratives for employees to use. In the narrative, each segment of the process (area of responsibility, movement of process steps, description of procedures, time line, documents, and internal verification steps) can be described in as much detail as required. The repetition of flowchart boxes aids in helping employees follow the flow and reminds them *where* in the overall process a series of steps resides. In Chapter 7, we provide examples of the combined narrative and process steps.

A DETAILED EXAMPLE

The example we use to demonstrate how problem solving evolves, is that of late shipments of products to customers. This example was introduced earlier in the book. The *initial* problem was expressed as:

> Sales reps promise customers that orders will be shipped within three days from placement of orders.
>
> This promise is not being kept by the Shipping and Receiving Department.
>
> The assignment: To improve the system so that orders go out within the three-day period.

We realize upon a fuller investigation that the problem is *not* isolated to slow processing in Shipping and Receiving. In fact, there are at least five distinct causes for the delay. To summarize the problems:

1. Sales reps do not always deliver order paperwork on time. In some instances, delivery of orders has occurred even beyond the three-day deadline.

2. The Marketing Department often does not process orders on the day they are received; in many instances, the delay extends at least two days.

3. Inventory records are unreliable. No one actually knows what is on hand and records are not accurate. An excessive volume of back-ordered products causes further delays.

4. Shipping and Receiving does not order its basic shipping supplies until they run out. As a consequence, they often cannot ship products on time.

5. The shipping supply vendor has refused to ship additional supply orders until prior month billings have been paid. The Accounting Department is frequently late in payment of bills due to its batch cycles.

Collectively, we face a far larger problem than the most obvious one. These five major causes of delays have to be addressed. In the thorough Six Sigma process, it is also likely that upon examination, a team will discover that the problems extend far beyond the apparent ones. For example, it could be discovered that the Marketing Department or Inventory Control departments suffer from deeper inefficiencies, and a revamping of entire systems might be necessary.

To demonstrate how a Six Sigma team would approach and solve this problem, we will create a horizontal flowchart of the process as it functions today, identify weak links and inefficiencies in the system, and propose changes in the following areas:

✔ Sales rep promises to customers and routing procedures

✔ Marketing Department processing system

✔ Accounting Department batch cycle adjustments

✔ Shipping and Receiving supply inventory procedures

These four areas do not represent the entire problem. For example, we would probably need to closely examine inventory systems and propose entirely new methods for counting, tracking, and ordering products. We may discover further problems in all of these areas. However, our purpose here is to demonstrate how the team proceeds from definition of problems through to identification of ways to increase Sigma levels. So we will limit our investigation.

Key Point If a problem expands beyond the original team mandate, it makes sense to indicate the need for a more extensive, detailed project—while remaining focused on the immediate problem as a first step.

Our first step is to better define the scope of the underlying problem. Addressing this in each of the four major areas:

1. *Sales rep promises to customers and routing procedures.* The initial promise of three-day delivery may be especially problematic. For example, orders taken late in the day on Friday cannot possibly be shipped by Monday. The Marketing Department and Shipping and Receiving employees are not available over the weekend. Initial examination of this starting point leads to a recommendation of a fine-tuning of the promise itself to:

> Orders taken before noon will be filled and shipping within three *business* days.

> Orders taken after noon will be filled and shipping within four business days.

The second part of the problem involved the routing procedure itself. Some sales reps were not delivering orders immediately to the Marketing Department. What is needed here is some formalized procedure to ensure that orders are routed immediately. The Six Sigma team may recommend an online routing order form, so that the additional step of *routing* the orders is no longer necessary. If the sales rep needs to fill the order on the automated system, this eliminates the need for the additional step. Without going into the specific system details, the Six Sigma team is aware of many affordable alternatives already available to sales reps. For example, e-mail updates and product information is available for download in the field. Sales reps could use the same system for order submission. This sub-project may be the topic of an additional task for a team involving Sales and Marketing departments.

   2. *Marketing Department processing system.* Currently, orders are often delayed because the Marketing Department does not get around to processing them for up to two days. This also means that Inventory and Shipping and Receiving departments often do not receive orders until the day of promised delivery (or later).

   If the sales rep procedure were automated, the Marketing Department procedure could be as well. The only purpose for routing an order through Marketing is so that sales activity can be closely monitored, tracked, and supervised. However, that should not affect the timely delivery of goods. The solution to the problem of routing is to develop a system that begins with order input from the sales rep that next goes into the system viewed by Marketing; and also routes the same information into an Inventory Control system *and* to Shipping and Receiving. In other words, the current inefficient system should be replaced with a single, automated system that ties in with Marketing tracking systems, Inventory Control, and Shipping. (This proposal will require a separate Six Sigma team involving representatives from each department, coordinated by an expert in automated systems design. Thus, in the definition phase, it becomes evident that the purpose for this team is to define the problem in its entire scope and to make recommendations for fixing that problem by way of a revised automated order processing system.)

3. *Accounting Department batch cycle adjustments.* The problems in the Accounting Department go beyond the one experienced with payment delays for the shipping supply vendor. That is a serious problem. The vendor has refused several times to ship orders because a prior month billing was more than 30 days past due. Not only is Accounting inflexible about its policy of routing all payments through a twice-monthly payment cycle; it also delays certain types of payments beyond the next cycle, causing late payment situations.

The solution is to revise accounting policies themselves. First of all, payment terms should be honored in all cases. A "net 30" agreement means just that; payments have to be made in a cycle that places the check in the vendor's hands within 30 days. The Accounting Department cannot ignore the importance of its vendor relations or, more to the point, of viewing the vendor as one of its customers.

In addition, the Six Sigma team may propose augmenting the current twice-monthly payment cycles with two additional, smaller cycles, to ensure that all payment terms can be met. These minor cycles can also be employed for more timely payments of expense reimbursements and similar expenses. Currently, the system causes delays of two to three weeks in many cases, due to timing of cyclical processing. The team should recommend that the Accounting Department create two minor cycles in between their major payment cycles each month.

4. *Shipping and Receiving supply inventory procedures.* The final problem to be addressed at this phase is the lack of forward-looking policies in Shipping and Receiving. Invariably, the supervisor hears about the need for more supplies when an employee reports, "We're out of . . ." The departmental routine needs to be changed to ensure that the department always has a supply on hand that equals or exceeds the reordering cycle. For example, if it takes two weeks from the time an order is placed with the vendor, through the (revised) accounting payment cycle, to delivery date, then it is essential that the department have no less than a two-week supply of its essential materials on hand.

In revising the accounting policy itself, it is also likely that the vendor will be more willing to ship goods promptly upon receipt of order. Once the vendor begins to experience prompt payment, it will no longer need to hold shipments until those payments arrive. This will facilitate a more rapid receipt of shipping supplies, making the whole procedure work more efficiently.

Key Point In identifying a fix for a particular problem, we often identify secondary benefits—like greater flexibility among vendors when payments go out on time, for example.

We have not addressed the specifics of the proposed new system that would carry through from order placement to inventory control and shipping notification; that is beyond the scope of this project, but certainly represents the ultimate solution to the problem of order fulfillment. In addition, instituting a more efficient and comprehensive automated system will enable the company to manage growth more readily. As long as sales reps are free to concentrate on meeting their quotas and placing orders on-line, the rest of the system will operate smoothly as well.

THE FLOWCHART

To translate these four ideas into flowchart form, the Six Sigma team begins with its defining tools such as the CTQ and, from there, begins to identify the sequence of events. In constructing the flowchart, it will be necessary to interview people in all involved departments; to specifically locate variance points; and to then develop a two-step summary. The first step is a flowchart showing the procedure as it works today, which is essential for coming to an understanding of the scope of problems within that system. The second step is a flowchart proposing how the system will work after changes have been put into place.

In this situation, given the proposal for a new automated order placement/inventory/shipping system, it may require considerable time to gain approval and to then develop the system. So the Six Sigma team may also propose interim steps to reduce variances and defects in the system.

The first step in the flowchart showing how the system works today involves order taking and routing to the Marketing Department. We call this process "Sales Orders." The following steps are involved:

1. Sales rep completes the order form.
2. Sales rep forwards each day's order forms to the Marketing Department.
3. The Marketing Department records order information. (Other tasks are performed as well; but for the purposes of tracking orders, we concentrate only on one aspect, how orders move through the system.)
4. The Marketing Department forwards orders to the Shipping and Receiving Department.

A flowchart for this first step in the current system is shown in Figure 6.3

The second phase involves Shipping and Receiving and its involvement with the Inventory Control Department. We have named this process "Inventory Orders." It includes these steps:

1. Shipping and Receiving receives orders from the Marketing Department.
2. Products are summarized on an inventory requisition.

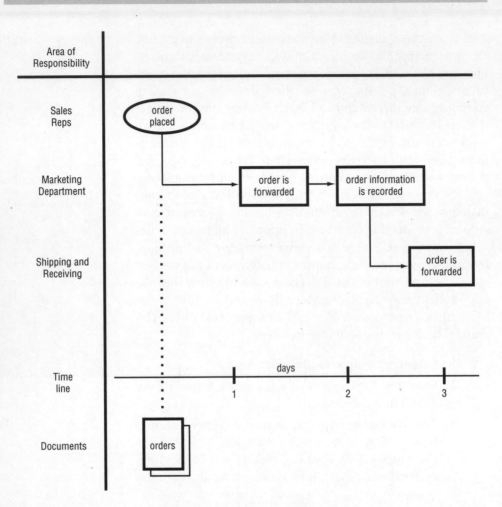

FIGURE 6.3 Sales orders flowchart.

3. The requisition is sent to the Inventory Control Department.

4. Inventory Control finds items on the requisition.

5. If items are not on hand, this is noted on the return copy.

6. The requisition is returned to Shipping and Receiving with products that were on hand.

7. Inventory Control back orders products from the production warehouse. (Tracking systems are involved, but are beyond the scope of this product.

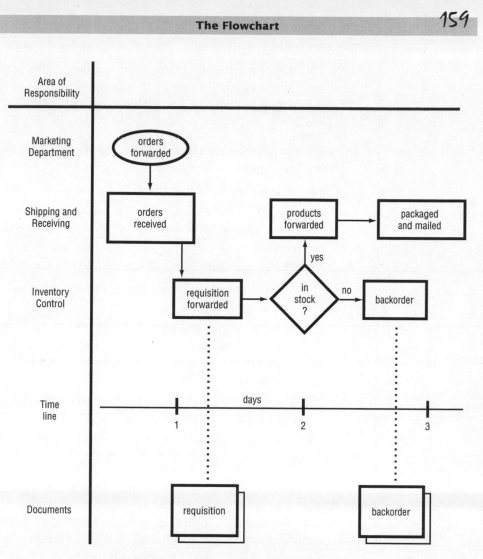

FIGURE 6.4 Inventory orders flowchart.

Back ordered products present a different problem that needs to be addressed via improved inventory control procedures.)

8. The products to be shipped are forwarded with a requisition copy to the Shipping and Receiving Department.

9. Orders are packaged, processed, and sent out.

A flowchart of this phase of the process is shown in Figure 6.4.

A third phase the Six Sigma team studies in this procedure is the reorder policies in the Shipping and Receiving Department, which we name Shipping Supply Process. Steps are:

1. Employees retrieve shipping supplies from the storeroom.
2. When supplies have run out, the employee notifies the supervisor.
3. The supervisor places an order with the supply vendor.
4. The vendor takes one of two actions:

   If payments are current, the order is processed and sent.

   If payments are past due, the vendor advises the Shipping and Receiving Department that shipment cannot occur until payment has been received.
5. The Shipping and Receiving Department notifies the Accounting Department.
6. The Accounting Department checks status and processes payment within its cycles.

The flowchart for this portion of the process is shown in Figure 6.5.

The final stage studied as part of this project is the Accounting Department policy and its cyclical timing. We use the name Accounting Process. The steps in the current procedure are:

1. Invoices and statements are received in the Accounting Department.
2. The Accounts Payable employee checks math and matches invoices with purchase orders.
3. Invoices are matched to monthly statements.
4. The costs or expenses are coded by the Accounts Payable employee.
5. A payment order is completed and presented to the supervisor for approval.

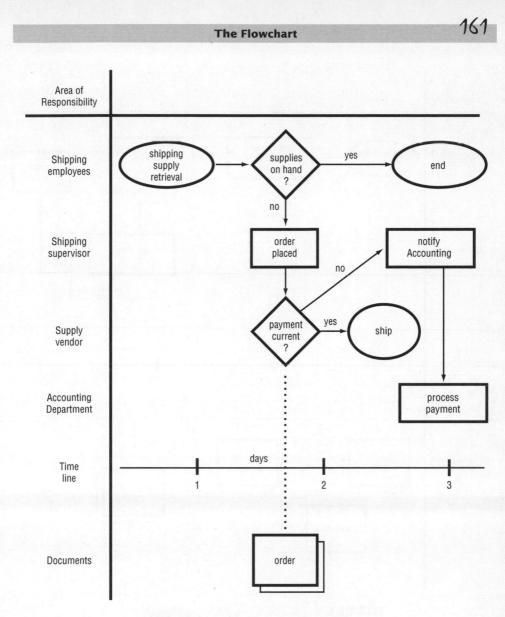

FIGURE 6.5 Shipping supply flowchart.

6. The supervisor checks coding and documentation and approves payments.

7. Payment is scheduled for an upcoming payment batch cycle.

8. If no discounts are offered, payments are delayed for 30 days from date of supervisor review.

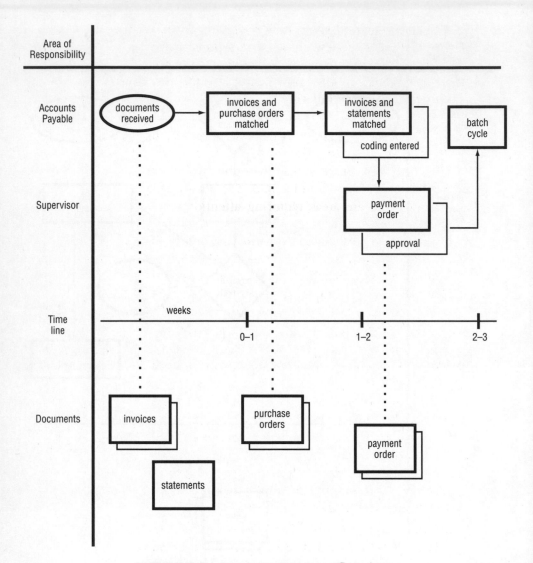

FIGURE 6.6 Accounting process flowchart.

9. Payments are processed in twice-monthly accounting batches.

10. Payments are mailed.

This process is summarized in the flowchart shown in Figure 6.6.

We have limited the scope of these flowcharts intentionally. The purpose is to show how a process is analyzed. From this brief overview of the current process, we have identified several variance points. By fixing these, we will be able to eliminate all the known defects in the current procedure. These weak links are:

1. *Sales Orders.* Weak links occur whenever work flows from one area of responsibility to another. This four-step process has two obvious weak links, between steps 1 and 2, and between steps 3 and 4. These are areas requiring attention. The first, forwarding orders from the sales rep to marketing, has to be changed to ensure that orders go in immediately. The second, the process of forwarding orders to Shipping and Receiving, should take place *separately* from the need to record data in Marketing; that will save a lot of delay time.

2. *Inventory Orders.* The weak links in this phase occur at virtually every step of the way. This indicates that the process is both inefficient and full of potential defects. The Inventory Control system is not working, evidenced by the fact that no one seems to know whether specific products are in inventory or not; and the high volume of back orders. While interim procedures need to be improved to fix this chronic problem, the long-term solution is an improved, automated inventory system that ties all stages together.

3. *Shipping Supply Process.* The biggest problem in this phase is the fact that supplies are not ordered until the department has run out. This prevents timely shipments. A procedure is needed to have adequate supplies on hand for a period no less than the time lapse between ordering and receiving new shipments.

4. *Accounting Process.* The accounting process is naturally slowed down by the need for methodical paperwork matching, coding, and approval procedures. These internal controls are essential. The problem here involves up to three weeks' delay to

conform to twice-monthly batch cycles. The system should be augmented with the addition of two minor batches in between.

Key Point   Identifying all the potential variance points is the first step in reducing defects—this is the key function of the Six Sigma team.

The process used in this example has now gone through preliminary definitions, CTQ, identification of likely variance points, and potential defects. Some initial ideas to fix the interim problem lead to a further recommendation to replace the current system with a broad, updated and automated program to help sales reps move their orders directly through the system. In the next chapter, we take these four brief examples and show how they can be combined with narrative for training purposes.

Chapter

Striving for Consistency

An especially complex series of projects were completely documented using a horizontal flowchart. In order to explain to employees how it worked, the flowchart was taped to the wall of the conference room. The Start point was clearly marked just to the left of the entrance to the conference room. The sponsor, a manager named Ryan, knew he was going to have a long day when the flowchart spread all the way around the room. He ran out of wall before he ran out of procedure. It became a joke around the company; the long string of white paper full of boxes and arrows came to be known as Ryan's Belt.

One difficulty your Six Sigma team will have in developing new procedures is going to be how you communicate your work to others. Your changes will affect everyone, especially those who will be directly involved in the process. In these instances, a long and complex process should be broken down into a logical series of smaller processes. This makes the idea of change more digestible. People have problems with change as it is; you lose a lot by trying to create too much change all at once.

It helps to develop new and improved processes when everyone remains focused on the keys to customer service; recognizes that everyone deals with customers in all their functions; and adopts the philosophy of Six Sigma by operating to improve that service in every way possible.

Even with a positive attitude and acceptance of team participation, you are going to run into some people who will resist change. It is normal. So the way that you design a new process or change an old one is only half the battle. The other half is getting your improvements to work smoothly and as quickly as possible. For that, you need cooperation from other people. You also need to invest in the development of training tools, which serve the added function of a selling tool. In the act of selling your ideas to management as well as to those who will need to change how they work, you will need to present convincing arguments.

THE KEYS TO CUSTOMER SERVICE

In the development of a new and improved system, it is essential to constantly keep in mind the priorities for tracking and designing that system. These priorities can be divided into four groups: prediction, communication, quality standards, and delivery.

Key Point Prediction, communication, quality standards, and delivery—the primary priorities to improving system processes—are the pivotal elements of customer service at all levels.

Prediction

In order to be able to reduce the occurrence of variances and the defects that they cause, we also need to install predictability into work processes. This is difficult in situations where the output is intangible, or where the variables themselves cannot be easily identified. On a production line, a defect occurs when (1) the unit does not operate or is incomplete, (2) the production goal is not met, or (3) the raw materials are not available. All of these are predictable and precise. But many people do not work on production lines; they are found in service operations, or in areas where the potential variables that may occur are elusive. For example, how do you identify variables in a purely service environment? What if the customer finds the service acceptable, but not exceptional? What if the delivery date is missed, but not by very much? Are these quasi-defects? Are they acceptable? Is the variety of possible defect levels so subtle that we cannot identify them precisely? All of these questions point out the problem with finding predictability in a service environment.

With this problem in mind, we need to set specific performance standards and make those standards part of the process itself. In the last chapter, we talk about identifying weak links by decision points, loops, and places in the process where work moves from one area of responsibility to another. These are good starting points for developing predictability. If we also impose time deadlines and standards, then we will be able to prevent most forms of defect. In the service environment, monitoring success can be difficult because it is the smooth operation that results from elimination of possible defects. We cannot point to specific units of production and demonstrate how improvements have occurred. We have to accept the fact that we can promise outcomes with greater confidence. "The report will be in your hands no later than Monday" is a promise you know the department can keep, because the process has built in predictable time variance standards. By way of example, this is a form of placing a quantifiable value on a defect (late delivery of a report) and developing a means for measuring its success. "How many times this month was a report delivered past the promised deadline?" would be the question. The answer would give us a measurable Sigma value. If we impose similar predictable measurements on other intangible operations, we can achieve the same quantifiable measuring capability.

Communication

A lot of emphasis is placed on how we convey information to one another. In corporate communication, we are supposed to deal with "I need," "You need," "They need," and similar beginnings to phrases—as opposed to "When are you going to get me what I need?" The old standards, like the use of the nonaccusatory "I" messages, the popular but impractical "One minute manager" school of thought, and other communication techniques, all lead to the same end result: Effective communication reduces variances, improves service, and allows everyone to work well together. When we consider the goals of Six Sigma as well as the overall philosophy behind it—that the corporate culture itself can be improved—we realize that effective communication is essential. A process works better when everyone knows what to expect from someone else as well as what someone else expects from them. In fact, finding variances and preventing them from turning into process or output defects, requires effective communication. In identifying variance-likely decision points and weak links in the process, also consider how communication may affect the variance levels, and how communication can be improved to prevent those variances. It may be a matter of improving a form, redesigning a report, or simply clarifying instructions, training materials, or deadlines.

Quality Standards

The best understood of the priorities is the one relating to quality. In the origins of "quality control," quality referred specifically to productivity and defect-free units of production, those tangible, measurable outcomes that make the concept of quality so specific. How do we establish quality standards in a service environment? How do we identify and monitor quality when our customer is internal? In dealing with end-user customers, one way to measure quality is to experience attrition. Dissatisfied customers go elsewhere. But if the service provider is the Payroll Accounting Department, the dissatisfied customer (everyone who gets a payroll check) has no choice but to deal with that department. Since there is no selection capability by the customer, several quality standard questions naturally come up: Does the service-providing department even need to make changes? How can the internal customer make his or her voice heard? How can Six Sigma help to improve a service quality problem? By identifying the elements of good or bad quality, the answers become apparent. These include timely delivery (see next priority), accuracy, responsiveness, communication, and style, among other possible elements. By listing the customer's expectations just as we would for an end-user customer, the whole service attitude changes. We do not want to lose our end-user customer because our corporate survival (revenue and earnings) depends on keeping that customer. So we need to transfer the same keen customer service attitude over to the internal customer; to increase quality within the organization; and to recognize the essential need for quality at all levels and in all interactions.

Delivery

Timely delivery of a product or service has always been considered the bottom line of customer service. It is essential. In Chapter 6, we deal with a multidepartmental Six Sigma project that began with this very problem. Sales reps promised delivery within three days from order placement. We discovered a number of factors that expanded the original question: Why can't Shipping and Receiving send orders out on time? to a far more expansive series of questions, including:

Is the three-day promise realistic?

Are sales reps getting orders in to Marketing each day?

Does the Marketing Department delay the process in its own handling procedure?

Do we need to improve inventory control systems?

Are the problems experienced by Sales, Marketing, and Inventory Control part of a larger problem, which may be solved with an integrated order processing and inventory control program?

Should Shipping and Receiving change its procedure to ensure it has basic supplies on hand in advance of the date they run out?

Should the Accounting Department make accommodations for more timely payment of vendor statements?

Key Point Any serious study of processes, including the issues preventing timely and complete delivery, will prove that thorough study and analysis are needed to permanently fix what is wrong. No one minute solutions are going to work.

In studying the components of the *delivery* question, we discovered—as is often the case—that the original problem could not be addressed with a singular fix. The "One minute manager" approach would not work. The problem did not reside in Shipping and Receiving alone; in fact, the problems in that department were relatively minor and easily corrected, compared to the overall problem of how orders were moved through the system.

PROMISE AND FOLLOW-THROUGH

In an attempt to further define customer service, we can equate the concepts of promise and follow-through—if only as a means for measuring the effectiveness of processes. We may also ask what the purpose is to trying to improve our internal processes; how and why the ideal of follow-through is so important; and how we can apply these concepts to intangible workflow.

Since we seek variances as a means for identifying problems, we also need to identify what actions have to be taken to reduce the occurrence and to prevent defects from growing out of the process. In most discussions of quality control, no distinction is made between variances and defects; they are considered synonymous. We have used two separate definitions to demonstrate how charting a process can work effectively. A defect, any outcome that does not meet the customer's expectations, is an outgrowth of the variance. We can locate the variance and prevent it from continuing through the process, thus preventing defects. This is the goal within the Six Sigma approach to quality.

We seek variances within the four priorities we have already identified: prediction, communication, quality standards, and delivery. The concept of "promise and follow-through" includes these priorities at each stage along the way. Six Sigma involves a lot of specialized visual concepts, process abbreviations, and teaching tools, all designed to help members of a Six Sigma team to arrive at the same definition for all the priorities. We predict, communicate, set quality standards, and deliver at some level for each and every process. The degree to which our promise is delivered defines the effectiveness of processes and, ultimately, the success of the Six Sigma effort to reduce variances and defects.

The first step is predicting even the most intangible of outcomes. By being aware of the need to define the outcome, we force ourselves to arrive at defining measurements of a process. For example, when a particular service process is undertaken, we *predict* the outcome in terms of many other items. For example, if we look again at the process for moving sales orders through the process, what is the predicted outcome? Putting it another way, what can we predict as the *desired* outcome? This distinction is a form of setting goals. For example, we could draw up a list of desired outcomes:

Sales reps are able to promise shipment of goods within three business days.

The Marketing Department will review daily sales orders each day.

The Inventory Control Department will receive orders each day.

Inventory Control processes will be able to track products and ensure they are on hand.

Shipping and Receiving will receive orders on the same day they are placed.

Shipping and Receiving will have no less than two weeks' supply on hand of shipping materials.

Accounting will ensure that all vendor bills are paid within 30 days.

Vendors have the right to expect to receive 30-day payments without exception.

These predicted outcomes define the goals of the project. They are reasonable goals, assuming that an automated order entry and inventory control system can be put in place. All of the involved departments and people have to ask additional questions about these goals. Among these are:

Is this set of desired outcomes realistic?

How will my job change if these goals become possible?

Will I spend more time or less time on the process?

Each individual and department has to assess the current process as well as suggested changes to determine whether efficiency is going to change (and in what direction), what extra costs or cost savings will result, and how predictable service levels will be improved.

Key Point   Every project is going to be defined by time, effort, and cost—not just in Six Sigma, but for every change made within your company.

These defining elements of the process—having to do with time, effort, and cost—have to be used as the defining elements for all internal dealings. We know that management measures internal efficiency in terms of revenue and earnings, so each and every process should be changed with that in mind. It should be possible to improve efficiency and service levels and, at the same time, reduce the cost of providing service. This is a respectable goal to set, and once we allow the creative efforts of team members to take off, virtually everyone will be surprised at the ways that prediction can be turned into a profitable ideal.

Within every process, the second priority—communication—can be improved in the majority of cases. We know that sections, operating units, departments, and even individuals, do not always want to communicate and when they have to, it is often minimal. The reluctance of people to communicate effectively is one of the chronic problems that Six Sigma is designed to do away with, so that everything works more smoothly.

For example, do we need to cancel out each and every variance? Do we need to prevent *all* defects? Practically speaking, we cannot achieve Six Sigma all the time. But under the definition of communication, we may improve service levels when we also improve communication. Some examples:

✔ The Inventory Control Department discovers that it does not have products on hand, even though an order has been received today. By communicating with the sales rep, the variance and defect may be mitigated. Because the sales rep promised shipment within three days, the new information is valuable. The rep may contact the customer, explain the situation, and apologize. Many of the examples in which customer expectations are not met lead to anger or frustration as the result of poor communication or even the complete lack of communication. The rep may further promise to keep in touch with the inventory situation, and promise that as soon as new products are received, the customer will be on the top of the priority list. In fact, the sales rep may even promise to hand-deliver the product. This is an excellent alternative promise with follow-through, giving the customer *exceptional* service in compensation for not being able to keep the original promise.

✔ The Accounting Department did not process the shipping supply vendor's statement during the latest major payment batch. However, realizing their mistake, the department has placed a telephone call to the Accounts Receivable Department of the vendor company, and has promised that the check will be going out in the current week's (minor) payment batch. In this situation, the vendor is likely to ship out a new order even though payment was not received as expected, because the company communicated the variance and offered an alternative promise.

In these two examples, the variance could not be undone; it was unavoidable. However, the importance of the defect can be defined by how it was handled upon discovery. We do not have to simply accept defects as failures in the system; with effective communication, we can reduce the impact of the variance on the customer. In this way, we offset a failed promise with a new promise and follow-through.

Quality standards also have a version of promise and follow-through. Again referring to the traditional production line, each shift promises (or sets a goal) to meet a production quota expressed in numbers of total units or numbers of defect-free units that will be produced. If and when those goals are met, the shift was successful. This same level of quality standard can be applied to service departments. The delivery deadline is the most dependable method for judging quality level for service, assuming that quality control also is applied to accuracy of content, presentation, and other important elements. The dependability of a service department, to be counted on for timely completion and delivery—especially of accurate, high-quality work—is a true test of how well the process is controlled. A failure in quality can invariably be traced to a variance that was not captured *during* the process and corrected before it caused errors, delays, and other defects. The promise is made in terms of accuracy and deadline; follow-through is measured and controlled by monitoring how well the promise can be kept.

Key Point   There is no secret to reducing defects. Simply catch variances as they emerge and prevent them *during* the process itself. The in-process efforts made by the people doing the work, is where variances are stopped, or allowed to continue.

Finally, delivery itself can also be measured when service is provided to an internal customer, or when the effort produces service rather than product. The promise of delivery most often relates to time; like the promise of quality as measured as a quality standard, we can also test delivery in a number of methods. For example, is the promise for delivery at 6 A.M.? Did goods show up later the same day? Is it more serious if they show up an hour late or a day late? If goods show up early, is that *better* than on time? If the product is perishable, early delivery can represent as serious a defect as late delivery. So by definition, the attributes of "good delivery" have to be defined as forms of promise: day and time, the number of items (if a product), and the quality. For example, if your shipment of cooked items gets to the retail store several hours late, only two-thirds of the order is filled, and the prescribed recipe was not followed, there are at least three defects. The promise has not been kept. Follow-through of delivery is perhaps the most complex of the four priorities, because so many variables can and often do affect the ability of the people and departments involved to ensure compliance. In these situations, the problem should be communicated to the customer, at the very least. For example, "Your cookies are going to be late because our oven broke" could be followed by an alternative promise: "We have found another oven we can use for the emergency, but it's smaller so we can deliver only half the order." This adjusted form of delivery—partial delivery—would be acceptable in many situations. Customers tend to become upset when they were given no advance notice of a problem. So if only half an order shows up, a report is not available at the time of an important meeting, or a check is not mailed by a promised payment date, then delivery promises have not been kept. However, if the customer receives an explanation with an alternative promise, it restores confidence. It tells the customer that (1) you are aware of the promise,

(2) there was a problem, (3) there is an alternative, and (4) *your* promise is a high priority.

MAKING THE FLOWCHART EFFECTIVE

Is it enough to identify likely variance points on the flowchart, if we take no specific action upon discovery of those variances? The Six Sigma process is not only a *system* by which processes are studied and changed; it is intended to work to create permanent improvements by upgrading the overall quality level. In a practical application of this idea, process analysis requires identification of a string of promises (which may be viewed as the service provider's mirror image of the customer's expectations). That process has to also include action steps, the communication of the problem to the customer if the deadline or other specific requirements are not going to be met. It is preferable, of course, to prevent the problem from turning into a defect through internal controls; but we know that this is not always possible. Ovens blow up, supplies run out, and produced goods can and do come out in a defective form. So in those instances where variances were not caught, processes should include mitigation measures.

This is a new idea in the traditional quality control world, where defects are absolute. A unit is either produced on time or not, and it is either acceptable or defective. There are no standards for "kind of okay" or "sort of on time." However, in the service world and when working with the internal customer, defects can and do come in shadings, some serious and others merely irritating. Six Sigma goes far beyond the statistical measurement of Sigma itself; the process also involves developing a concern for the real service level with the idea that problems can be solved and the way that things work can be changed. So even when defects do occur, we want our processes to reflect a serious commitment to service, and we want customers to develop confidence that either the outcome will show up on time and in the condition expected, or—failing that—an alternative will be offered that will be acceptable in the majority of cases. So Six

Sigma is not always going to expect an outcome to be 100 percent perfect or 100 percent defective. The *real* service level, and the *real* quality level, are going to be more intangible than that, and may involve perceptions about service just as much as service outcome itself. We may have one situation in which customers usually get their products or services on time but have very little confidence in the company, and another with opposite attributes: a higher rate of late delivery but greater customer confidence. It depends on the philosophy that the company brings to the Six Sigma process, and in how well employees pick up on it and put the ideals into action.

Key Point   Real service and real quality often are found in how we respond to discovered defects, and not so much in preventing those defects completely.

The process itself, once outlined on the horizontal flowchart, has to serve as a working model of the process. You will probably go through this flowcharting procedure at least twice: once to show how work flows today, and another time to propose improved methods to achieve the same process but with fewer variances (and with better internal controls). At the same point that variances are likely to be discovered, you may also build in worst case scenarios for how to proceed when variances cannot be avoided. When your oven blows up, for example, you need a back-up plan. Effective flowcharting, no matter how thorough, cannot anticipate every possible disaster in the process. However, it can identify the most likely points where such back-up plans are going to be required.

In addition to documenting and highlighting these likely points, it is a worthwhile effort for the team to further consult with the person or department executing that phase. "What happens if . . ." questions may be followed by "And then what can you do?" so that the process can identify the plan B actions that will be needed to offset the problems. Once the responsible person begins to think in terms of variance discovery and prevention as well as back-up planning, the rate of potential variances and defects will fall dramatically.

The question of how the shadings of quality can be upgraded are not going to take place on the flowchart. These changes have to reflect a change in overall attitudes toward service and, because these are intangible, it is difficult to measure them. In fact, the idea itself is a hard sell. It is always going to be difficult to present ideas to Management without a well-based set of assumptions about how decisions are going to affect profit or loss. You cannot go to Management and claim that improved service attitudes, even in the face of defective outcomes, is going to dramatically change the customer's perceptions and translate to profits. Or can you?

Remember, in the *traditional* Management style, "quality control" is viewed as something that happens in the plant, the assembly line, or on the warehouse floor. It does not climb the stairs to Management's domain. Six Sigma, on the other hand, cannot exist or succeed unless it begins in Management's domain; so the need to improve quality on all levels, including how discovered defects are treated, is a matter of immediate interest to Management. If the service attitude goes all the way to the top, then Management will appreciate the subtlety of defect response. Their appreciation for the importance of this aspect of quality will be immediate, because everyone in the Six Sigma environment recognizes the limitations of measurability. We can measure only so much; we have to take some of the improvements we design on faith. If we know it works but we cannot put a value on it, that does not mean it should be ignored. So initiating quality improvements even after a defect has occurred is an important element of the Six Sigma approach to quality, whether talking about a small, isolated process or a company-wide application that affects everyone.

THE NARRATIVE/PROCESS DOCUMENT

All the work we undertake to fix defective processes has to be explained to management, to the Six Sigma sponsor and leadership council, and to the employees involved in the process. So given the limitations of measuring intangibles, we need to build a flowchart and narrative explanation to demonstrate (1) how processes operate today, (2) where variances occur, (3) how and why those variances lead to defects, and (4) what those defects look like. Within this process, we may discuss intangible variances or post-defect handling and response; however, in addition to this, we need to also be able to convey the problems of the current process.

Second, we need to be able to demonstrate how suggested improvements in the process make it more efficient, save time, and reduce cost. We also need to be able to show that the flowchart highlights likely variance points, while recognizing that we cannot possibly find all of them. If we locate most likely variance points, we will experience a dramatic improvement in overall quality, a rise in Sigma.

Key Point   Combining graphic and narrative information is perhaps the most powerful way to convey information, to prove your point, and to train and inform others.

Third, we need to design our flowcharting document so that it also serves as a training tool and instruction manual. The more processes are changed, the more you are going to need to document the methods under the new process. Some flowcharting techniques call for presentation of a flowchart and a narrative procedures manual, and these are expected to be useful in combination. In practice, though, employees experience difficulty in translating the graphic and the narrative. Considering that the employee referring to the manual is not certain about what to do, why, where to get raw material, or what to do with it, a complex flowchart is going to be more intimidating than helpful. With this in mind, the narrative/flowchart combination is the most effective method of training.

Some guidelines for combining graphic and narrative documentation:

✔ *Keep it short and simple.* A training or procedures manual has to be designed on a step-by-step level. No matter how familiar you are with a process, the person looking at your documentation is on new ground. Break down complex processes into shorter, smaller steps and explain them methodically.

✔ *Explain the key elements: sources, processes, outcome.* In every process, there are three primary stages. Something arrives, it is processed, and it goes somewhere. The new employee may not understand any of these elements. While a procedures manual is normally involved with process steps, the employee might be concerned about the questions: Where does it come from? and Where do I send it when I'm done?

✔ *Include form samples.* Forms and other documents used in the process, or produced as part of the routine, should always be included. Filled-in forms are the most useful, especially when the documentation provides a thorough example and shows how data is transferred onto the form itself.

✔ *Highlight weak links and explain how to operate internal controls.* If we expect to reduce variances, we have to tell the person doing the work (1) where they are most likely to occur, (2) how to prevent or correct them, and (3) what to do if variances cannot be fixed. The way that essential steps operate are how internal controls succeed or fail.

✔ *While providing detailed information, also provide the big picture of why this process exists.* Perhaps the greatest flaw in job descriptions and procedures manuals is that they emphasize steps in the process, without explaining why the process exists. Every segment of your documentation should begin with an introductory short paragraph that places the process in a logical context.

The purpose in preparing documentation is ultimately to help employees perform processes in the intended sequence, and utilizing the internal controls designed within that process. Initially, though, documenting the process is a method for demonstrating inefficiencies and variance points. In fact, it is unlikely that you will be able to recommend improvements until you have first documented the entire process as it is performed today. Once you have the document in hand, it is far easier to make recommendations to fix variances and to eliminate defects. In fact, during the process of flowcharting a process, some of the problems will be obvious, and fixing them will be an easy matter. The intangibles, on the other hand, will have to be accepted as likely secondary benefits to fixing the major sources of variances. In other words, if you eliminate the obvious and tangible variance points through redesigned internal controls, the process will then involve far fewer instances of intangible service issues. Post-defect response will be less of a concern when pre-defect variance prevention is shown to work well.

Key Point   Flowcharting provides numerous benefits. Among these is the possibility that you will discover variance sources previously not recognized by anyone else.

Besides requiring you to thoroughly document the procedure (1) as performed currently and (2) as you propose to change it, this exercise is an excellent way for the Six Sigma team to work together, pool its expertise, and develop a single version of their recommendations. Just as individual employees can easily get lost in the complexities of a flowchart by itself, or in the pages of a training manual without graphics, a Six Sigma team member can also be overwhelmed. Each team member is going to start out understanding only a small portion of the overall process; the team's overall responsibility is to develop a complete understanding of how the process works and how it can be improved. This requires transforming the team member's focus from an initial isolated, myopic point of view, to a broader, executive-level overview of the problems and opportunities in changing the process. So the Six Sigma experience is an exceptional tool for expanding team members' horizons and training them to think in more visionary terms.

THE GRAPHIC/NARRATIVE DOCUMENT

Your Six Sigma team is probably going to need to document processes in two ways: as currently performed and as changed. In both of these instances, the graphic flowchart can be combined with a narrative description to help others understand the process itself. While both graphic and narrative forms have their limitations, the combination of the two is an excellent means for explaining a process. Whether you are presenting your ideas to a leadership council or sponsor, or providing it to employees as a training tool, the combination of both is the best means for communicating ideas.

In the previous chapter, we break down the sales order system into four primary segments: sales orders, inventory, shipping, and accounting. To demonstrate how the graphic/narrative process works, we concentrate only on the first of these, the way that sales orders are processed. We show a graphic/narrative document for the system as performed currently, to show how this combined document may appear. From this, alternatives can be proposed. For example, in the case of order processing, the Six Sigma team would propose the design of an automated order entry system to make the whole timing of orders and inventory work more efficiently.

To begin, let us review the procedure as it is performed today. A graphic/narrative version of the current procedure is shown in Figure 7.1. While the graphic portion of this comes from a horizontal flowchart, the narrative custom is vertical, so we break down our steps in a vertical presentation. A reviewer, accustomed to reading from top to bottom, is provided with the additional visual aid of each step in the process.

This format makes it easy to refer from the big view of the horizontal flowchart to the detailed instructions found in the narrative description of the process. It also provides context for the reader; it is easier to see where

Sales Order Flowchart

Purpose: This section describes the process used by Sales Representatives in placing orders, forwarding those orders, and following through with customers.

Step 1: The order is placed. The order is forwarded.

The Sales Rep completes the order form, provides the customer with the first copy, retains the second copy, and forwards the original to the Marketing Department. All orders are forwarded or delivered on the day the order is placed. If the Representative is unable to ensure receipt by the Marketing Department, the details are to be called in to the Marketing Department by telephone.

Step 2: Order information is received and forwarded.

The order is received in the Marketing Department. Information is recorded from the order form on Sales Rep records, on current product sales tracking records, and on regional sales goals records. A copy of current order volume is forwarded to the Regional Manager at the end of each day.

Orders received each day are forwarded to Shipping and Receiving and to Inventory Control for fulfillment.

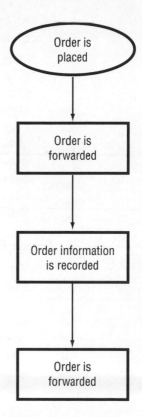

FIGURE 7.1 The graphic/narrative document.

the step is in relation to the overall process, a valuable feature not available in the purely narrative training or procedures document.

Key Point It is imperative that team members, managers, and employees be exposed to the big picture of the process. Without this context, you cannot expect anyone to appreciate the need for change. Six Sigma teams need not only to figure out how to make things work; they also have to be able to convey this information to others.

This single page can be used to explain to Management exactly how the procedure works today. It can serve as a generator of discussion points, identification of weak links, and interactive discussion for how the process can be improved. Ultimately, it will lead to development of a more efficient system. The stages identified on the sales order flowchart, combining graphic and narrative steps, is only the starting point; but it specifically identifies what gets done, who does it, and what potential variances can grow from the system.

The biggest variance in this procedure, and the most obvious, was the inability of the company to ship products within three days. The flaws in the system are many. Some of them are visible on the figure; others would come out in subsequent documentation. The point, though, is that as a means for fixing the problems, this format is going to be useful as a powerful tool for translating Six Sigma theory into an effective action plan.

Chapter

Exceptions and Rules

A friend was thinking of selling a house without using an agent. A local real estate agent talked her out of it, explaining, "When it comes time to close escrow, you will need me there to guide you through the paperwork." Of course, by the time the deal was finalized, an escrow agent organized the paperwork; in fact, the agent didn't even show up. "It's all right," the escrow agent told my friend, "We don't need her to be here."

By whatever definition you use, *service* means meeting expectations and requirements. If a real estate agent convinces a customer that the 6 percent commission they get is money well spent, it should be based on something. If the agent is able to bring more potential buyers to look at the house, that is one form of service. If the agent advises the seller on how to fix up the house to make it more attractive, that helps, too. But providing false information or, more to the point, playing on the seller's fears, is a very negative form of service.

You never know how poor service is going to come back around later. In the example at the beginning of this chapter, the friend who sold her house ended up investing in numerous other rental properties; her sales commissions went to a new agent, because she realized that she had not been well served. The original agent's integrity was clearly lacking, so that agent lost a good customer. Even without the lost business element, good service should be provided as a matter of sound morality. We find that in business, as in all other things, an example of good service is most often also the right thing to do.

EFFICIENCY VERSUS COST

The "right thing to do" is not merely a statement about morality; it is also a part of your job description. If you are paid to process information, deliver packages, or prepare reports, your employer deserves to have expectations and requirements met. In fact, your performance is going to be measured by how well you provide the expected and required service. So the right thing to do is the same as good service, and it is the same as good performance on the job.

Key Point You will often find that "doing the right thing" is the same as "performing your job well."

Once the entire organization understands this premise—the cultural philosophy of Six Sigma and the underlying service ethic of the quality program—everything changes. People begin to see service opportunities in everything they do; they begin to see customers everywhere they look; and they recognize how small changes often make a big difference in how work progresses.

Another aspect of this change in point of view is related to efficiency. There is a common belief that "things have to get done quickly to save money." This is the most irrational and provably false belief in the corporate culture. In fact, forcing processes to move too quickly leads to errors, dissatisfied customer reactions, and spending *more* time and *more* money getting it right later on. When a customer feels rushed by a retail clerk because a lot of people are in line, it is an uncomfortable feeling and that customer does not want to come back. When a bookkeeper rushes through a posting routine, the input gets transposed and the books do not balance; another half day is spent trying to find the mistake. If you rush a report without checking research and double-checking your math, errors and inaccurate information go into that report, and the person who finds it (and someone inevitably finds it) will have no confidence in your ability to "do the right thing" within your job description.

Faster is not cheaper. It is more expensive, and the deliberate, methodical, self-defined pace of a routine has to be respected and followed. If shortcuts are taken, that results in more variances and more end-product defects. The belief that by moving faster, we save money is contrary to what logic tells us.

Any analysis of a process has to include the time element in addition to the steps involved, the area of responsibility, and the documents that are produced. In an assembly line environment, rushing through a process is known to cause delays, more defects, and higher costs; the same is true in the purely service environment as well. A manufacturing process studies the assembly method and recognizes—in fact, looks for—likely weak links, those points where variances are most likely to occur. The most likely causes of defects are employees not paying attention, going too fast, and not checking their own work. These problems should sound familiar, because they are the same problems found in all processes. People in service departments, even purely administrative in nature, can learn a lot from the quality control problems and solutions of the manufacturing environment. The idea of transporting the production-specific quality control approach into offices and service companies has always been revolutionary, in many respects. Some people have ridiculed the idea; others have tried to apply it incorrectly.

In the 1970s a fad hit service industries—the hiring of efficiency experts. These consultants often were the corporate equivalent of the Feng Shui culture that became popular in the 1990s and remains in vogue today, to some extent. Just as the efficiency expert might have brought a level of validity to the analysis of process behavior, the Feng Shui consultant may be able to offer valuable insights about home or office design. But depending entirely on such consultation is a mistake. The efficiency expert who attempts to identify, down to the minute and second, how long a specific function took, was unable to appreciate the variables of service as an intrinsic part of that service. Things do not always take the same amount of time.

So as a form of trying to quantify process—much like the One Minute Management school of thought—the idea just did not work.

Key Point Efficiency—on a practical level—has to mean more than just cutting costs and getting things done more quickly. Otherwise, it is just a word.

The approach to quality control in a service environment was too often based on ill-conceived concepts of efficiency. In a plant environment, an efficient routine can be identified in such terms: producing a unit takes x amount of time, and may involve y number of variables. This analysis can be placed on a grid and studied visually; patterns emerge and can be studied; and efficiency can be taken down to the minute and second. Service is not the same as production, and processes take a wide variety of time, depending on far too many elements to reduce to a chart. For this reason, many people viewed quality control as a joke. Management often allowed quality programs to be put in place just to respond to calls for involvement and participation. Some imposed standards: "Prove you can save money and I will support the program." So quality control programs were invariably geared toward cutting costs and expenses (often meaning layoff increases), and the typical employee came to fear the concept of more efficiency—knowing it could result in their losing their jobs. Management also failed to realize the importance of top-to-bottom involvement in quality, and treated such programs as ideas to be put in place at the departmental level.

So in the evolution of quality control from our past, which was essentially a manufacturing economy, to our present, which is more of a service economy, the appearance of Six Sigma has been a substantial change from the quality programs of the past. The complete participation by top management, exemplified by General Electric's past CEO, Jack Welch, makes Six Sigma different from the types of quality control systems proposed by efficiency experts, and from the magical fix-all proposed by environmental specialists such as Feng Shui consultants. There is nothing magical about Six Sigma. It is hard work but it produces very real results. Not only are processes improved through more efficient work; those participating in the change also benefit from the Six Sigma approach.

So the concept of "efficiency" has to be examined carefully. It does not mean doing things more quickly, getting out a higher volume of work, or moving a customer through the line with less delay. It does mean identifying variance points and developing internal controls to prevent defects. When the efficiency expert of the 1970s reported to Management, the conclusion often came down to judgments about time. If a particular set of employees was costing the company a specific salary level per month, that expense could be cut by an assumed percentage if employees could only work more efficiently. So when Management took the advice of the efficiency expert and cut employees, the message to everyone else was: "Work harder and faster, cut the time out of processes, and be more efficient, or you, too, could lose *your* jobs."

Ultimately, this approach led to inefficiency, lower morale, and a universal fear and loathing of efficiency experts. After all, it was unheard of for an efficiency expert to find no flaws in processes, or to advise keeping all employees on staff but improving that intangible service. The efficiency expert did not know how to explain the value of improved service, the universal customer, or the competitive advantage to improved processes. So the obvious solution was to propose a demonstrable cost and expense savings. If the efficiency expert could convince Management to cut $6,000 per month from payroll, that more than justified the one-time consultant fee of $3,500, for example. If we hire an expert witness to tell the jury that a client is insane, that witness—paid to come to the conclusion—is going to convincingly cite various forms of proof to support the contention. The efficiency expert was a type of expert witness who, tragically, lacked any real expertise other than the ability to manipulate numbers. The motivation of the expert—to justify what the company was paying for the advice—required that some immediate offsetting benefit be identified.

For anyone who has been involved in the analysis of

processes and who understands how variances evolve, the idea of speeding up work or reducing employee numbers, is clearly contrary to the best interests of the company. In a manufacturing environment, efficiency does often equate to employee layoffs. When Boeing's orders for 757s drop, a segment of the manufacturing work force is laid off. A few months later, when orders pick up again, the same people are rehired. But we cannot improve internal service provisions by telling employees they have to speed up their work.

THE INVISIBILITY OF THE EFFICIENT SYSTEM

Quantifying efficiency is easy in the manufacturing plant. A shift meets its quota with minimal defects, which is an acceptable outcome; another shift falls far short of units produced, and the number of defective units is higher than average. This is an unacceptable outcome. The units of production, defective units, and expectations are based on precise measurements.

Key Point Efficiency in the production of tangible goods is fairly simple to identify. But an efficient service is, by its nature, invisible. The more efficient, the less we see it or even think about it.

In the service environment, such outcome-based expectations are not as easily measured. By definition, service is intangible. A word processing clerk meets a specific work load and is known to be highly accurate, whereas another one is slow and makes a lot of mistakes. While we recognize the difference between these two employees, how do we place a numerical value on the varying levels of quality? In some respects, the high-quality work of the first employee is invisible. It is defined by the absence of problems.

This raises interesting challenges for the Six Sigma team. Since the merits of a quality program are invariably measured in terms of results, how does Management determine that a project has succeeded? Was the team's effort worthwhile? Were expenses reduced? Was customer service improved? All of these questions serve as the basis for comparing one quality approach to another. In the best-designed system, however, high quality is going to be invisible. So how can the Six Sigma approach be measured?

The team is expected to perform a number of testing steps and to develop internal controls, specifically designed to stop variances. If, a few months later, no variances are occurring, how do we know that these internal controls are even necessary? We need to be able to measure the effects of variances by assigning a measurable value to defects, which come in many shapes and sizes. The larger the volume of opportunities, the more varied the forms of defects; so when internal controls are working, we may be aware of fewer defects without really knowing why.

The Six Sigma team needs to define its goals in a way that can be measured. These measurements have to include:

✔ The difference made by installing internal controls, by tracking variances (even those variances that do not end up as defects)

✔ Defects of various types, employing a before and after study of outcome based on what are assumed to be effective internal controls

✔ Defects by degree, meaning the level of impact a defect has on the customer and how we react upon discovery (referring to the post-defect response time, effort, and attention, recognizing that customer service has a reactive side as well as a preventive side)

✔ Means for determining the effectiveness of the team effort

In each of these instances, the team needs to develop measurable changes made by the work it undertakes. In setting goals during the early definition stage, the team needs to define, quite specifically, what changes it expects to see. For example, if the problem in a particular process is defined as time delay, then one goal would be to reduce late delivery without incurring additional costs and, at the same time, without increasing variances and defects. This is all quite measurable. The three elements of the defined problem to be solved are:

1. *Time delay* is very measurable. If a particular process, such as shipment of orders within three days, is taking six to seven days on average, any change in the average can be counted easily. In fact, an analysis of time delay as a Sigma of the process is a good way to judge the effectiveness of other process components (automated order entry system, inventory control, and changes in internal procedures in Shipping and Accounting departments, for example). As the Sigma of time delay changes, we can judge the overall effectiveness elsewhere. So as the average shipping day approaches three days, that particular variance is reduced and finally all but eliminated. This is a good example of how to measure results; the particular problem is complex and involves many individuals and departments. Ultimately, though, improvements in the process are going to translate to a better record in shipping orders.

2. *Cost reduction* (or keeping costs at current levels) does not always serve as the most important element of a project, although some projects are specifically geared toward identifying the causes of overruns, and changing the process to eliminate them. One mistake often made in quality programs is to impose a requirement that a cost element has to be involved. However, cost is a good method for offsetting other means of measuring outcome. For example, if the order processing system can be achieved within three days but the costs are huge in comparison to the current system, it is appropriate to ask whether the additional cost is inevitable and necessary. Cost increases are not always inevitable or necessary and, in fact, in system improvements, we often find that costs are reduced as a natural outgrowth of the efficiency gained. So measuring cost—even if the goal is to maintain at current levels—is also an effective measurement of how well the Six Sigma project has worked. For example, in a presentation meeting, if questioned about the cost element, it is desirable for the presenter to be able to tell Management, "We have reduced defects by half and increased production time, with no increase in cost."

3. *Reducing variances and defects* is clearly a primary concern for the Six Sigma team. Even so, these are not easily measured. This is why time and cost are valuable methods for at least a part of the overall measurement. However, if you know what constitutes a variance or a defect, you will certainly be able to judge the results of a changed process. Even though the efficient system is invisible, the claim can be made that variances and defects that commonly occurred in the past have been entirely eliminated. (This never means that Six Sigma has been achieved, but it does mean that the chronic problems have been caught by new internal controls.)

WHAT CUSTOMERS REMEMBER

A customer is going to remember how he or she was treated. This is true, of course, for both the external (end-user) customer and for the internal customer. When a customer brings a defect to your attention, the way you react is going to be what the customer remembers. If you take the message as a problem, if you are reluctant, or if you do not take full responsibility, then the customer's experience will be negative. This is far more important in the long term than the defect itself.

Key Point Most customers understand that things sometimes go wrong. But they will not forgive being treated as an inconvenience when they complain. That is the greatest service defect of all.

As part of the process analysis you perform on a Six Sigma team, be aware of the importance of post-defect response. Although the customer service attitude is an intangible aspect of the whole process, it is among the most important. When customers are treated badly at the point of complaint, it is the most serious of all defects, because that impression remains with the customer or, we may more accurately say, ex-customer.

Example The Customer Service Department for a credit card company had assessed a high interest rate on a customer's bill. However, a six-month introductory no-interest period was in effect. It took the customer several phone calls before the problem was resolved. In the last phone call, the customer service rep argued with the customer and denied responsibility for the problem. The discussion went something like this:

Customer: I just want this problem solved, not only to remove the charges but also to make sure it doesn't happen every month.

Service rep: It only happened on one statement.

Customer: Yes, but what I'm saying is that your mistake caused—

Service rep: Wait a second, *I* didn't make a mistake.

Customer: I didn't mean you personally, I meant the company. I don't want to have to deal with this again next month.

Service rep: If you had mentioned the promotional period when you first telephoned, this whole matter could have been cleared up much faster.

Customer: I did mention it.

Service rep: Well, we can only fix a problem if you tell us exactly what it is.[1]

We can see many, many aspects of this conversation that could have gone better. If the service rep was more aware of what has to be done in a customer service environment, and would also be able to take responsibility for the error, it would have been a far more positive experience. For example, the conversation *should* have gone like this:

Customer: I just want this problem solved, not only to remove the charges but also to make sure it doesn't happen every month.

Service rep: I understand, and that's a reasonable concern.

Customer: Your mistake has caused me to have to spend hours on the phone trying to get it fixed.

Service rep: I'm very sorry for that. It was our error and you shouldn't have to spend your time.

Customer: I just don't want to have to go through this all over again next month.

Service rep: I promise you this won't happen again. I've flagged your account and updated the automated file. I can assure you, this was an isolated error and you won't have to deal with it again.

In this example of how the conversation could have gone, the customer service rep did the three things in each response that should take place in every service contact, especially when a customer is complaining. Look at the responses again. The service rep empathized, apologized, and promised. These are the elements that should apply in every complaint situation.

Example You have been waiting for a statistical report from one of your company's subsidiaries. You need the report in order to finish a study you are doing, and your deadline is approaching. Finally the report is delivered, but it is three weeks late. You telephone the supervisor to remind him that there is a second report you need, and that it is supposed to be submitted two weeks from today. The supervisor could say: "Hey, we had a lot of other stuff to do and this report put everyone behind. We'll try to get your second report out, but I'm not making any promises." Or, if the supervisor considers you his customer, he might say, "Of course I know you have a deadline to meet and I apologize for getting this out to you late. I promise the second part will be there by the deadline, absolutely."

You are, of course, likely to react more positively to the second message. The first one was hostile and essentially accused *you* of delaying the department's work. It was *your* report that put everyone behind, after all. Nothing productive can come from such an exchange, whether internally between departments or externally with end-user customers, vendors, or subcontractors. The more positive approach, based on a commitment and a promise to fix the problems, goes a long way to building trust and confidence. Equally true, a negative attitude in which the customer service rep does not take responsibility, only augments the problems and creates resentment and mistrust.

The Six Sigma philosophy—apart from the technique itself—helps everyone to take on a new point of view concerning service. Whether your company makes a distinction between contact with customers and internal interactions, or considers it all to be the same, the underlying philosophy is what makes this approach more powerful than that used in other customer service regimes. In too many cases, "customer service" means listening to complaints and fixing them in some way: product replacement, discount coupons, a half-hearted apology, or a promise that the problem will not be repeated. In this environment, you end up with employees exhausted by an unending stream of accusations, anger, frustration, and resentment. In a short period of time, those employees become demoralized and their tone changes. They no longer emphasize, apologize, and promise. Instead, they accuse, deny, and react. They accuse the customer of somehow causing the problem ("You didn't mention the special condition"); they deny responsibility ("I didn't make a mistake"); and they react to the problem ("We can only fix a problem if you tell us what it is") instead of figuring out what is causing it and then fixing it once and for all. In the reactive Customer Service Department, the tone itself creates more distrust and resentment among customers than there would be if there were no response at all.

Key Point What is worse, no response to customers or a very negative response? The customer may shrug off silence, but will never forget the rude customer service representative. Never.

A Six Sigma customer service approach is much different from the traditional one. Instead of waiting for complaints to arrive, Six Sigma teams look for variances and come up with methods to prevent them from occurring. A variance in its most common form never has the chance to become a defect because it is caught and stopped within the internal controls of the process. The root cause is treated rather than the symptoms. Second, the Six Sigma process would carry through to the post-defect complaint and then revisit the procedure. The purpose here is to go after the causes again. Is this a problem we missed? Do we need to change, add, or improve internal controls? What else can we do to make sure this specific defect does not happen again? Six Sigma is designed to ensure that you anticipate and prevent defects by looking for variances and eliminating them.

THE ABSOLUTE NEED FOR A HIGH STANDARD

Do we need a high standard in our interactions with others? Assuming that these interactions are variations of customer service, why does that standard have to be high? One common reaction among people when they first hear about Six Sigma is, "Perfection? That's impossible."

Of course, consistent perfection is impossible. But by being about to define what perfection means, we can accurately measure defect rates and how our team improvements reduce those rates. As you experience the Sigma rising in response to fixing variances, you come closer and closer to perfection. The purpose of Six Sigma is never to reach perfection, but to better understand what needs to be done to improve current processes.

Accounting budgets are the same type of process. The budget is intended to serve as a goal. In a perfect outcome, the budget states, "We believe it is reasonable to see these results." Too many accountants become concerned with the problem of variances, situations where expenses exceed the budget. The variance is viewed as a problem that has to be explained away, but the real value of that variance is that it gives an indication of where the initial assumption was flawed; what changes can be made today to curtail further variances; and how the entire budgeting process can be improved. In fact, the budgeting process itself would make an interesting Six Sigma process, because the natural progression of analysis would be likely to point out an entirely different set of problems and opportunities than might be assumed at the beginning. For example, the assignment might be to "figure out how to reduce expense variances." The *real* assignment might be more effective if expressed as "figure out how to use variance information to reduce expense overruns."

Example In one corporate Accounting Department, a monthly budget report included a budget explanation. For many years, executives had been satisfied with an explanation of what caused the variance. For example: "The 22 percent overrun in Office Supply Expenses was caused by excessive employee access to supply storage areas. The excess is expected to be absorbed gradually over the balance of the fiscal year." This explanation says, in essence, "Employees take supplies, we know about it, and we *think* we built this factor into the budget." It does not offer solutions. A more effective response might read: "The 22 percent overrun in Office Supply Expenses was the result of excessive employee access to supply storage areas. We have implemented a new procedure requiring requisition of supplies from a single employee, who maintains supply inventories in a locked storage area."

This revised example shows how the reactive explanation—employee theft, which will be absorbed in the remaining budget allowance—can be replaced with an effective internal control. This is the point to Six Sigma: It is not intended to simply improve processes or make them more efficient. It has the purpose of identifying the actual causes of variances and proposing solutions to stop them. So an original assignment might turn out to be invalid if the Six Sigma team discovers that the real problems are more complex. So the assignment to "get orders in the mail within three days" may evolve to a project to "revise the entire order processing and inventory control system; expand accounting payment cycles; and revise shipping supply inventory policies to ensure three-day turnaround of orders."

OVERCOMING THE PROBLEM OF THE EXCEPTION

Every systems person—the individual given the task of deciding how things get done—has an appreciation for consistency. The systems designer likes predictability. Of course, this makes systems work easy. The real challenge is in deciding how to deal with exceptions. This is so important because, in a practical application of a system, the *exception* often is what leads to a variance and, ultimately, to a defect as well. A three-day delivery promise might not be possible if a particular shipment has to be insured, shipped overseas, or packaged differently from the standard order.

Key Point   Exceptions cannot be avoided in any process. Actually, exceptions make work interesting. Do not forget the fact that "variety" and "variation" come from the same root.

There are three ways to deal with exceptions: by elimination, response, or process change. The most effective internal systems are those that anticipate and manage exceptions without causing problems (variances) elsewhere. In some applications, an exception naturally creates some form of variance that has to be acceptable because, by definition, the exception does not fit. The three methods often dictate how the Six Sigma team develops its project, remembering that exceptions cannot be allowed to alter the course of events for the majority of instances. Internal controls have to be set up to deal with exceptions, but it is a mistake to design the entire system around those exceptions. Some suggestions:

✔ *Elimination.* In some processes, the exceptions can simply be eliminated. However, remember the emphasis on service; be careful in deciding too abruptly to simply refuse to deal with exceptions. For example, if the Accounting Department refuses to process a reimbursement check or vendor payment until the next cycle, that may simply be too inflexible. But if someone wants to be paid in cash, given a check today while they wait, or have the check payable to Cash to avoid taxes on the payment, those types of exceptions must be refused and eliminated from consideration.

✔ *Response.* The service attitude favors response as the best method for handling exceptions. The exception is taken through the process as efficiently as possible and, if exceptions recur, the process could be augmented with a plan B process for frequently recurring paths. The minor cycles in the Accounting Department are examples of appropriate response; the two major cycles are augmented with interim minor cycles. This enables the department to continue processing most of its work without delay, while also accommodating those payment requests that arrive in between.

✔ *Process change.* If exceptions become so frequent that they are putting the process into unending chaos, that is a sign that the process is not working. It has to be changed. A new Six Sigma project needs to be undertaken, with the initial assignment to be to take a look at the process and recommend changes and greater flexibility.

In all of these methods of handling exceptions, emphasis should continue to be placed on variance identification and internal controls. The exception may be the starting point of a variance and can easily lead to a defect. Because the exception requires a different process from normal, it is one of the most important weak links in the system. You need to ask: How can the likely variances that grow from exceptions be anticipated and stopped? A second but related question is: What internal controls do we need to ensure that exception processing in an variance-free as normal processing?

Example In one company the accounting routines are fully automated with one exception. The books for a small subsidiary are maintained on a manual system during a transition. By next year, you expect to merge the existing system into the automated system. For now, however, a process is underway to post and balance the books by hand. Last month, the bookkeeper was out of balance by three dollars. The initial response was to say, "It's only three dollars. That's not worth spending hours and hours to find." So the posting error was not pursued. However, it came to light this month that the two-cent error consisted of two unrelated posting errors. One was exactly $100.00, a common posting error. The other error was a transposition. The bookkeeper posted $405.00 instead of $504.00:

First error	$100.00
Second error ($405.00 minus $504.00)	– 99.00
Net errors	$ 3.00

This is a case where the scope of the variance itself was underestimated. It is easy to make mistakes such as this. It also demonstrates why systems like bookkeeping are designed to *require* thorough testing and balancing. It is exact, and for a good reason. So a variance may also hide from you. In the preceding example, the problems may have been discovered in an executive meeting; the CEO might have asked the Chief Financial Officer, "Why doesn't this column add up? It's off by $100.00." That would be embarrassing to the CFO, of course, who depends on the CEO's confidence in the numbers; so a three-dollar variance is not acceptable in this situation.

Key Point   Sometimes what seems like a small variance is only the tip of the iceberg. It could lead to far more disastrous problems.

Emphasis on exceptions—like even a seemingly small out of balance condition—and on internal controls are the keys to increasing the Sigma level. The exception (a small out of balance condition) required further investigation. The failure of the internal control (not pursuing it because it was only three dollars) is where the system failed. So applying this to each and every process, we can discover where variances emerge and then devise ways to stop them.

It is never possible to completely remove the variances from a process. Human error, mistakes in going through process steps, exhaustion, distraction, and other factors are going to enter into the process. Most of these problems can be discovered through internal controls and fixed before the outcome takes place. But not all. We need to balance the exception with the practical, and even to accept some level of defect.

Many years ago, the manager of one department had a quirky rule for his employees: Every report had to be "paginated" without exception. That meant that every copy of every report had to be reviewed, page by page, to ensure three things: No pages were upside down, no pages were backward, and no pages were out of order. Many years before, a report had gone out with an obvious placement error. The manager had no faith in modern printing and collating methods, so he insisted on spending time to check everything, even when a report contained hundreds of pages and dozens of copies were printed. The same supervisor was in the habit of checking the math on computer print-outs, even though math errors never appeared.

The point here is an important one: While we cannot expect to achieve perfection, we also have to employ quality control systems with reasonable perspective. Six Sigma cannot ensure 3.4 defects per one million operations, and setting such a standard would be impossible to meet. A certain level of defects has to be expected in all situations. It may be possible that a modern printing system could place a page out of order, or that a computer could make a math error. Do we want to spend all of our time looking for remote possibilities like that? Or would we be better off ensuring that internal controls worked well? Six Sigma has two components, but both have to be applied with reasonable and realistic expectations. The technical systems aspect of Six Sigma involves how teams work together, what steps are taken, and what forms of analysis are used to make dramatic differences in defect occurrence. The philosophical aspect of Six Sigma, the change in the corporate culture, has to come from the company's leadership. You depend on your CEO to not only place Six Sigma teams throughout the organization, but to also accept direct responsibility to participate in the point of view: that service applies to everyone and to every process, and that by using Six Sigma, the company will be more profitable and more competitive; it will also find that its employees work better together when everyone has a sense of taking part, and in being on the team.

Glossary

area of responsibility the person, department, team, board, committee, subcontractor, consultant, or other individual or group, identified as having primary charge over one or more steps in a process.

Black Belt an experienced participant in the Six Sigma process, usually given the role of team leader, who is responsible for ensuring that the benefits of Six Sigma projects are realized.

BPM (Business Process Management) an approach to work based on a model (Business Process Model) describing how work moves from step to step through the organization.

business case a summary of the purpose to the project, its financial impact, and the problem the team intends to address.

coach the Six Sigma expert or consultant who sets a schedule, defines results of a project, and who mediates conflicts or deals with resistance to the program.

concurrent operations in a complex process, the involvement of two or more separate areas of responsibility, each performing a series of process steps. Concurrent operations may require linking back and forth between different areas of responsibility, or they may proceed separately until a point where the separate effort is united into a single, concluding series of steps.

CTQ (Critical to Quality) a sketch of the customer's expectations and requirements, showing the major stages, departments involved, and other important steps in developing a process that successfully meets a Six Sigma project's goals.

defect   any outcome that falls short of the customer's needs or expectations.

design requirements   the process elements of products or services, which may need to be adjusted to meet the customer's requirements.

DMAIC   the tactical approach to Six Sigma projects, involving five phases: define, measure, analyze, improve and control.

FMEA (Failure Mode and Effects Analysis)   A process for identifying likely defects before they occur, using a rating scale; the purpose is to identify areas where preventive measures will be useful in a process.

Green Belt   the sponsor or a key team member with a degree of experience above the average team member, or who plays a key role in helping the sponsor manage the scheduling and assignments within a project.

horizontal flowchart   a tool used to visually document the way that processes work; and to identify points where variances are likely to occur. The purpose of the flowchart is to help the Six Sigma team develop improved systems and suggest changes to reduce defects.

implementation leader   the person responsible for supervising the Six Sigma team effort, who supports the leadership council by ensuring that the work of the team is completed in the desired manner.

leadership council   the team or committee that defines the specific goals of a Six Sigma process, the provider of goals to be met by the team.

Lean Six Sigma (LSS)   a system combining the concepts of Six Sigma with those of lean manufacturing, a system designed to improve cyclical efficiency and reduce or eliminate waste in processes.

Master Black Belt   a consultant (sometimes the coach) available to the Six Sigma team to resolve technical issues or to answer questions.

process owner   the individual who takes on responsibility for a process after a Six Sigma team has completed its work.

process variances   the points within processes where variances emerge; such variances lead to process and output defects unless the process is altered to correct variances along the way.

project charter a document summarizing the important elements of the project: name, business case, scope and goals.

Quality Function Deployment (QFD) a conversion of processes required when a customer's requirements are not compatible with current operating procedures; designed to adjust those processes to ensure quality improvements.

scientific method a set of procedures used to objectively evaluate information, to arrive at an accurate conclusion based on initial assumptions, definitions, and tests.

sigma the level of variation compared to an average; the Greek letter, σ used by statisticians to denote standard deviation.

SIPOC a process map that identifies all the elements of a project: Suppliers, Input, Process, Output, and Customers.

Six Sigma a measurement denoting near perfection, representing six standard deviations or 3.4 million defects per million operations; the ideal against which actual performance is measured.

sponsor the problem solver within a Six Sigma project, usually a manager who implements the orders passed down by the council; often the process owner, or person who is ultimately responsible for completing a process.

stakeholder analysis a process in which the project team determines who will be affected by the outcome of a Six Sigma project.

standard deviation the degree of exception, or variation from the average, in a group of outcomes, used to describe exceptions to an expected result.

standard normal the normal distribution of outcomes based on a statistical assumption that a mean is zero and a standard deviation is 1.

team leader the individual responsible for overseeing the work of the team, and for acting as go-between with the sponsor and the team members; the person who manages the schedule.

team member an employee who works on a Six Sigma project, given specific duties within a project, and deadlines to meet in reaching specific project goals.

value chain   a series of activities required to effectively design, market, and deliver a product, service, or other outcome.

Voice of the Customer (VOC)   in Six Sigma analysis, information gained by observation of a customer's requirements and expectations; the true needs of the customer, as opposed to the assumed needs under which the company operates.

weak links   the specific points in a process where defects are most likely to occur, commonly points where a process passes from one area to another; where logjams occur; or where decisions have to be made.

Notes

Chapter 1 The Meaning of Six Sigma

1. George Eckes, *Six Sigma for Everyone*. Hoboken: John Wiley & Sons, 2003, p. 10.
2. Jack Welch, address at GE Annual Meeting, April 23, 1997.

Chapter 2 The Customer's Point of View

1. Milind M. Lele with Jagdish N. Sheth. *The Customer is Key*. New York: John Wiley & Sons, 1987.
2. James B. Cabell. *The Silver Stallion*. St. Leonards, NSW, Australia: Unwin, 1926.
3. Kenneth Blanchard. *The One Minute Manager.* New York: Berkley Publishing Group, 1983.
4. United States Senate Report 107–205, "Purpose of the Legislation," 2002.

Chapter 3 Outside-In Thinking

1. Eric Hoffer. *The Temper of Our Time*. New York: Harper and Row, 1967.
2. H. L. Mencken, in *Washingtonian*, November, 1978.
3. George Bush (Sr.), remark about the future, 1988.
4. Michael Porter. *Competitive Advantage*. New York: The Free Press, 1985.

5. Nicholas V. Iuppa. *Management by Guilt*. New York: Fawcett Books, 1985.

Chapter 4   The Nature of Quality

1. U.S. Navy, New London, Connecticut maintenance facility, 1985.

Chapter 5   Product and Service Defects

1. Jack Welch, address at GE Annual Meeting, April 23, 1997.
2. Tom Devane. *Integrating Lean Six Sigma and High-Performance Organizations*. San Francisco: Pfeiffer (John Wiley & Sons), 2004, p. 10.
3. In the parable, four blind men are asked to describe what an elephant looks like. The first touches a leg and says the elephant looks like a pillar. The second touches its side and says it looks like a wall. The third touches an ear and says the elephant is like cloth. And the fourth touches the tail and says the beast looks like a rope. Source: *The Buddhist Sutra (Parables)*.

Chapter 8   Exceptions and Rules

1. Telephone call between the author and a customer service department, March, 2003.

Index